SOFT SPOTS

SOFT SPOTS

A Marine's Memoir of Combat and Post-Traumatic Stress Disorder

CLINT VAN WINKLE

St. Martin's Press
New York

www.stmartins.com

Design by Phil Mazzone

Library of Congress Cataloging-in-Publication Data

Van Winkle, Clint.
     Soft spots / Clint Van Winkle. — 1st ed.
         p. cm.
     ISBN-13: 978-0-312-37893-6
     ISBN-10: 0-312-37893-9
   1. Iraq War, 2003—Personal narratives, American.
2. Van Winkle, Clint.   3. Soldiers—United States—Biography.
I. Title.
     DS79.76.V36 2009
     956.7044'373—dc22

                                                2008035767

First Edition: March 2009

10 9 8 7 6 5 4 3 2 1

What if none of it happened the way I said?
Would it all be a lie?
Would the wreckage be suddenly beautiful?
Would the dead rise up and walk?

—**W. D. Ehrhart,** *Beautiful Wreckage*

SOFT SPOTS

1

RUM AND COKE SPLASHED onto the tiled floor when
I bent down to pick up a dress blues blouse. The midnight-
blue top, with its high-neck collar, red piping, and thick white
cotton belt, had been tailored to fit snug around my trim body.
Things had changed, though, primarily my waistline, and it
would have taken some sort of divine intervention to get the an-
odized buttons anywhere close to their corresponding button-
holes. But that didn't stop me from trying.

No luck. I threw the blouse in the corner, rooted through
the rest of the uniform pile. A desert-patterned boonie cover
with a faded Marine Corps emblem ironed on the front was
one of the few items of clothing I knew I could still fit into.

I found the floppy-rimmed hat tucked beneath a pair of gabardine trousers, and slid it onto my head before finishing what little remained of the watered-down rum and Coke. "You're all fucked up," I said when I saw myself in the mirror. The bald-headed reflection staring back at me resembled the eighteen-year-old boy who'd showed up for training at Parris Island in 1997 more than it did the twenty-five-year-old sergeant who had commanded a section of amphibious assault vehicles during the initial invasion of Iraq. Sergeant Van Winkle, the Marine Corps martial arts instructor, had disappeared long ago and left behind an out-of-shape college student named Clint—a person I'd grown to dislike.

The first year home from war had not gone smoothly, and with the redeployment of my old unit imminent and my younger stepbrother Matt still a few months away from completing his first tour in Iraq with an Army Scout Cav unit, I couldn't help but believe that I was letting everyone down by hiding out in a university classroom.

After pouring a fresh drink, I walked down a short hallway to the office and sat in a swivel chair. In the clutter on the desk lay a dusty Ziploc bag that contained an equally dusty notebook. Most Marines carried the same green notebooks. The small hardcover books were almost as important as rifles and ammunition. With so many "moving parts," relying on memory was a surefire way to fuck things up. I took the notebook from the bag, flipped through its weathered pages.

February 14, 2003: the first entry. Corporal Shawn Kipper was sandwiched between Staff Sergeant David Paxson and me, stuffed uncomfortably into the middle seat of a Boeing 777 that the U.S. government had chartered to fly our battalion to Kuwait. Rifles and pistols were stored haphazardly in the overhead bins, mixed in with pillows and kiddy-sized blankets. Deuce gear—war belt with canteens, first-aid kit, and butt pack full of miscellaneous supplies—lay tangled like a pile of spaghetti around boot-clad feet. Openmouthed, resembling a pair of oversized flytraps, Paxson and Kipper slept.

According to the onboard navigation screen on the bulkhead in front of us, the Celtic Sea was thousands of feet below. I looked out of the window, wondered if I would ever again get the chance to see the region. Only a few faint lights were visible from my vantage point, but looking at them sparkle made me think of what it would be like to be in a different situation: trolling in a fishing boat in the choppy water below, wrestling heavy nets of fish out of the sea. We were flying across the world to free a nation, but I only thought about our freedom. It was Valentine's Day, but all I could envision was death.

"Welcome to Kuwait," the first sergeant said over the plane's loudspeaker. Jet-lagged and stuffed full, we gathered our weapons, deuce gear, and gas masks and headed for the exit. Heat seemed to press against my body when I made it to the door, as if it were telling me to think long and hard before stepping out into the blazing sun. I squinted, took a deep breath of the dry air, and followed Kipper down the gangplank.

"Peace out, fools," Paxson said as soon as our boots made contact with the tarmac. He raised one of his heavily tattooed arms in the air, made a peace sign, then jogged toward Headquarters and Support (H&S) platoon. He had to get there fast, to help his platoon sergeant stave off any mutinous/illegal/unethical activity and beat the unruly group of Marines into submission before they got anyone demoted, arrested, or killed. He would then have to take at least one head count, probably four, before the plane lifted off into the clear blue sky, to ensure that none of his H&S Marines had changed their minds and decided to ride the plane back to the States. It was unfortunate that a locked-on Marine like Paxson, who was respected by everybody, had to coexist with the H&S knuckleheads.

Kipper and I took our places in first platoon, an assemblage that made H&S look like a Girl Scout troop. Seeing Kipper standing diagonally in front of me, I realized that his squared-away uniform contradicted the plump body it covered. Out of shape and about twenty pounds away from being within Marine Corps height-weight standards, his physique didn't fit the description of a Marine. If you went by personal appearance alone, you might have concluded, incorrectly, that he was a dirtbag Marine or maybe even a mean-looking sailor—a hard-charging corpsman or crusty Seabee. But unlike Paxson, Gunnery Sergeant Yates, and me, all active-duty Marines, Kipper didn't have to be in Kuwait or anywhere near the place. He could've stayed home and watched the war on television like the rest of America, slapped a "Support the

Troops" magnet on the back of his lifted truck, and called it a day. We wouldn't have thought any less of him had he decided to stay home with his new wife; he'd already done his time. But he wasn't that kind of guy, and when Paxson informed him that the unit had received the warning order to deploy, Kipper didn't give it a second thought. He knew what *he* had to do.

"There goes our freedom bird," I said to Kipper.

"Yep."

"Regret your decision yet?"

"Ask me in a few months."

I stepped out of formation, looked down the row of Marines I was in charge of leading. Besides boot camp and MOS (military occupational specialty) school, none of my third-section Marines had ever been on active duty. They'd done the one weekend a month, two weeks a year routine up until that point. Even my active-duty experience was questionable. Neither a reservist nor a "regular" active-duty Marine, but a hybrid of the two and the bastard child of both, I'd spent three years in the reserves before signing a three-year active-duty contract to work as a member of the Inspector-Instructor staff at the very same Norfolk, Virginia, reserve unit. So, while the Marine Corps had been my full-time job, I'd never been in the fleet.

"Third section," I yelled.

"Yes, Sergeant," they replied in unison.

"Weapons in the air."

Twelve M16A2 service rifles. All present and accounted

for, I stepped back into formation, jotted down the number in the front of my green notebook. Staff Sergeant Sterlachini, the platoon's senior section leader, called the platoon to attention, then put us at rest. "Weapons high in the sky," he ordered. I raised my Beretta M9 pistol. He walked through the ranks, counted the number of weapons aloud, called everyone he passed a "cocksucker," and threatened to skull-fuck the entire platoon if we didn't keep our goddamned mouths shut. We could never tell whether Sterlachini would really do the things he threatened or if it was all lip. A crazy, unhinged look gave us the impression that the wiry staff sergeant was capable of just about anything.

I'd been in the Corps long enough to know that we would have to count weapons at least two more times before we were given permission to walk over to the ammo crates to collect ammo. Gunny Yates would get his count, then the first sergeant. After counting and recounting, a senior enlisted Marine would step in front of the battalion formation and point out the obvious in a lengthy safety brief. An anecdotal story or two about Marines who had done dumb things with live ammo would certainly follow the brief. I wasn't disappointed.

"Section leaders," Gunny yelled. "Take the boys to the ammo." The three section leaders posted behind the ammo crates. We doled out rounds to our Marines, ensured that each man received his exact allotment—thirty rounds of 9-mil for pistol carriers and sixty rounds of 5.56 for the Marines with M16s—and not a single round more.

I fingered the smooth tips of the 9mm rounds when I

finally got mine, slid fifteen of them into each of my two magazines. Receiving the ammo meant the operation we were about to embark on was real, not another training mission. No more shooting at paper targets or charging through the woods with blanks. We were going live. So I savored the rounds as they clicked into place, dreamt about all the things I might get to do.

A line of small white buses stopped behind our formation, sent a cloud of dust in the air that momentarily blocked out the sun.

"Sterlachini," Gunny yelled.

"Yes, Gunny," he answered.

"Get a head count and get 'em loaded."

"Which buses?"

"That *one*." Gunny pointed to the bus at the end of the column.

All thirty-eight Marines of First Platoon, along with our flak jackets, Kevlar helmets, two canteens, weapons, magazines, boxes of MREs, and crates of extra ammo, were expected to cram into a single "short bus" that wouldn't have been big enough to carry a class of kindergartners to the zoo. I stowed my green notebook in the back of my flak jacket, where the armor plate would've been inserted had it been issued to me, and flopped into the cumbersome piece of gear before trekking over to the bus.

All the gear weighed well over eighty pounds, but it didn't matter to us how much anything weighed. We were amtrackers, operators of amphibious assault vehicles (AAVs or amphibious tractors/amtracs), and wouldn't have to worry about humping anything anywhere once our platoon of tracked vehicles arrived in Kuwait. Each crew of three would hang their packs on the Gypsy Racks that ran along the sides of their assigned AAV, use cargo straps to secure even more gear to the top, and squirrel away the rest of their belongings in various places inside the cavernous troop compartment. The grunts (infantry) we would chauffeur into combat would be lucky to have as much room as on the short bus provided First Platoon. But a squad of them would scrunch into the back of each AAV and make the best of a situation none of us had any control over. Regardless of how much room the grunts were given, riding in the back of an amtrac was better than humping a pack through the desert or being transported around a war zone in a soft-sided, seven-ton truck.

Even though an AAV resembled a tank to many civilians, and looked menacing enough to take one on in a firefight, the boxy vehicle was more bark than bite. With just a .50-caliber machine gun and MK-19 40 mm grenade launcher in each turret, it lacked the firepower to slug it out with an outdated Iraqi tank. Still, grunts were always thankful for whatever made their jobs easier, even if it was a platoon of lightly armored vehicles. They'd gladly sit on the three skinny benches in the troop compartment and choke on the exhaust fumes that would inevitably stream down through the two open cargo hatches. They would find ways to cope with being tossed around like a bunch of ball bearings in a spin cycle as the vehicles bumped their way through Iraq. The grunts would complain, but they'd still be thankful.

The "haji" bus driver smiled at me when I entered the bus, as he'd done for each Marine who had walked on before me. For him, a group of young U.S. Marines with loaded weapons, an elevated level of testosterone, and not the slightest clue on how to tell the difference between an Iraqi and Pakistani seemed enough to keep him jittery. Whatever his ethnicity, few of us knew it, which gave us enough reason not to trust him.

Sergeants and above commandeered the front. Corporals plunked down in the aisle seats. Everyone else squeezed their asses into whatever leftover space they could find. Gunnery Sergeant Yates, our platoon sergeant, stepped onto the bus. He refused to cram in next to anyone and stood in the doorway, to the right of the driver, literally riding shotgun. Gunny Yates had a first name, but nobody dared to utter it, afraid the all-knowing Gunny would somehow hear "Jerry," and then start wearing Marines out for blaspheming against him. To us, he was "The Gunny," and that was as personal as we were allowed to get with the former Parris Island drill instructor who had never fully left the drill field. Larger than life isn't an adequate description of Gunny, who could easily have been a character in an action movie. With a voice reminiscent of Dirty Harry and a temperament that would have made Godzilla seem pleasant, it was easy to imagine the man living in a different era, holding up stagecoaches or robbing banks.

While we knew we'd suffer under his command—would train harder and endure more ass chewings than the other platoons—his hardness was comforting. Marines complained about him, but never about being in his platoon.

Gunny ordered us to pull the blue velvet curtains tight across the shut windows, which immediately transformed the cramped bus into a rolling sauna. Taking drags off the exhaust pipe would've been more refreshing. Now that we were all loaded, another weapons count was taken—still all present and accounted for. Gunny leaned out the door, gave a thumbs-up to the lead bus. "Shut the fucking door. We're rolling," he told the driver. The driver looked puzzled and didn't seem to understand what he was being ordered to do. He spoke English, somewhat, and probably understood three of the four words Gunny had barked at him. "Shut. The. Fucking. Door," Gunny repeated.

The caravan of buses crept forward. I peeked out of the curtains, watched the land pass by in clumps of indistinguishable shades of brown and tan. No trees, no desert bushes or cactus, just rolling hills of smooth sand. Sweat collected in the creases of my forehead, slimed around my helmet straps, down my neck, and into my olive drab skivvies shirt. Kuwaiti police cruisers drove erratically through our convoy, forced oncoming vehicles onto the shoulder of the road, ran others into the median.

Kipper, who was seated behind me and apparently studying the strange land through his porthole, too, tapped my shoulder. "See that?" he asked. Five Bedouin men in long white robes and checkered head scarves walked into the desert. They appeared to glide over the ripples of sand as they moved away from the road, swinging long, skinny sticks at a herd of camels. The animals did what they were told and pushed deeper into the wasteland.

Twenty minutes of nothing but dirt, until a berm lined with several strands of concertina wire appeared in the desert. "All right, boys," Gunny said. "Grab your trash and police your areas." The dirt mounds marked the outer perimeter of Camp Matilda. None of the Marines seemed impressed with the camp's name. We'd heard the surrounding camps had names like Camp Commando, Camp Coyote, Camp Ripper, and Camp Iwo Jima. Those were exciting names, names you could write home about.

One of the largest bases in the Kuwaiti desert at the time, Matilda took its name from the Australian folk song "Waltzing Matilda," which also happened to be the official march of the First Marine Division. The camp, we would later find out, was a lot cooler than Camp Commando, a base mainly composed of REMFs (rear echelon motherfuckers), like the reserve battalion commander who ended up residing in an air-conditioned tent, not far from a Baskin-Robbins ice cream stand.

The buses stopped next to a wooden guard tower, at the beginning of a gravel road, just inside the camp. A couple of Marines armed with M240 Gulf machine guns occupied the structure and barely gave us a second look as we unloaded. They hadn't been in country for more than a few weeks, but I knew they were up there saying something about the "fucking newbies."

Formation. We took another head count (still all present and accounted for), and then stepped it out in formation. Each step stirred the desert loose, causing Marines to gag as gas masks bounced against hips and weapons gathered crud.

It only took a few minutes to realize that Matilda, by Marine Corps standards, was a five-star resort. With several shower trailers, four chow halls, and rows and columns of massive tents that rivaled anything Barnum and Bailey had ever plopped into place, it was much better than anything a Marine in a combat MOS could've hoped for. If Camp Matilda was the Greatest Show on Earth, we were the parade of animals marching through the camp in our clean cammies.

Gunny called cadence, navigated the platoon down the gravel road and past a legion of blue Porta-Johns that stood between the berm and the road. The aroma of week-old shit and sun-boiled sanitation water was less than welcoming, but at least we knew we wouldn't have to dig holes in the desert yet—not that any of us had a problem taking a dump in the wide open or squatting over a hole in front of the entire Division.

"Platoon halt," Gunny ordered. We stopped. "Left face." We turned, got our first look at where we would be living while awaiting the word to move twenty-five kilometers north to the Iraq-Kuwait border. Two platoons per tent would make the quarters as cramped as the bus ride had been and only slightly better than living in the sand. "When I give the order to fall out, you will go inside the tent and ground your gear in an expedient manner. *Fall out.*"

Plywood floors creaked under the weight of our overburdened bodies. We moved as fast as we could, found spots we deemed appropriate for our rank. First platoon sergeants and above dropped gear in the front of the tent, beside a pair of cloth flaps near the north entrance-exit. Paxson and the rest of H&S platoon did the same on the south end. Sergeant Camacci, Second Section's leader, and I secured an area next to one of the flaps on the right side of the tent. Kipper dropped his gear beside us. The Gunny hogged an entire corner on the left side. Nobody attempted to be his neighbor.

"Nice and tight, close it up, get away from my stuff."

"Aye, aye, Sergeant."

Even though the sun had yet to fall below the horizon, we assembled our beds: dropped gray foam ISO mats down onto the floors, unfurled black Gore-Tex sleeping bags, and molded gear from our packs into pillows. Without unpacking anything else, and one more weapons count, a Marine tied the cloth entrance flaps shut and turned off the overhead lights. I crawled into my bag, pulled my notebook and pistol in with me.

Our platoon of twenty-six-ton AAVs was parked in the well deck of a Navy ship floating around somewhere between Camp Pendleton, California, and Kuwait. Normally, trackers ride along with their vehicles, then splash them off the back of a naval vessel and "swim" the vehicles from the deep water to shore. The ability to move from ship to shore carrying a full complement of battle-ready troops and gear made us unique among all branches of the military. Amtrackers epitomized the mission of the United States Marines Corps, and we knew it, making us a cocky bunch of Marines.

Not having any AAVs to train with was a minor detail to Gunny. He marched us into the heat and sandstorms anyway. With or without our amtracs, we were going to train. So, while the rest of the company goofed off in the tent, Gunny had First Platoon pretending we were actually in AAVs, walking through formations and immediate-action drills. He even ordered each AAV to simulate a turret by having its crew chief extend an arm out like it was a loaded .50 cal as the drivers and rear crewmen marched behind their Crew Chief calling out targets and ambushes. To top it off, and to give it an even more realistic feel, Gunny made the rear crewmen, who were holding on to the shoulders of the drivers in each of the three-man conga lines, move their arms in a downward motion each time we stopped. Dropping a bent arm toward the deck was supposed to symbolize the lowering of an AAV's ramp, which covered the back of the vehicle, and indicate the debarkation of the grunts, who would run off each vehicle while the crew chief spun his turret around and fired rounds downrange. It was fucking crazy, and we looked like a band of morons kicking around the desert with our arms poking out, acting like we could shoot rounds out of our fists. After a few of those training missions, Non-NCOs started humming as loud as they could, imitating the roar of an AAV.

"YAT YAS," Gunny yelled.

"You ain't tracks. You ain't shit," we replied. False motivation was still motivation. Gunny could play that game, too.

Twenty-five kilometers and several weeks away from war, the Marines had already started to become homesick, lovesick, and nervous—anticipating Dear John letters; bored with the sun-drenched days of prepping and Gunny's endless slave driving. The mixture of feelings hovered over the camp like a cloud of mustard gas. With each passing day, the outgoing mailbag got heavier. Headphones and writing relieved me of the monotony of camp life, offered a brief reprieve from the surroundings. Others gambled, flipped through dog-eared smut magazines, and slept. When we weren't training, we sat around. The waiting was killing me. All I wanted was a war.

I listened to a Dave Matthews Band song called "The Space Between." Staff Sergeant Sterlachini let me borrow the CD, which I kept. I'd traded him a pair of desert boots for three cans of Kodiak chewing tobacco and felt he still owed me a little for the boots. The song, used in the *Black Hawk Down* movie trailer, seemed more than fitting as we waited in Kuwait, stuck in the space between combat and home. Still, neither Dave Matthews nor his band would've enjoyed knowing I was using their song to psych myself up for war. I turned their love song into my war song. I was thinking about sending rounds downrange, watching bodies hit the dirt, and where I would be hiding, mentally, when all that happened. Where would I take my thoughts in order to accomplish the mission?

I lowered the volume on the CD player and looked up from my journal. The tent was breathing from a sandstorm. It inhaled, exhaled, pulling and throwing dirt everywhere. Scraps of paper that had been pressed against the outside of the tent blew in. Lance Corporal McDaniels ran over to the entrance and tied the cloth flaps shut again.

It was much quieter inside the tent than usual. Most nights the tent resembled, and sounded like, a casino. But that had given way to a somber tone. While most of us who had been around the Corps for a few years knew that eventually we'd get a speech about dying, the "death letter" speech the company first sergeant gave in morning formation still seemed to take the platoon by surprise.

We'd been told it would be a good idea to write a "death letter" in case we didn't make it home alive. The first sergeant said we should write the letter to our loved ones: wife, children, parents, or whoever. It didn't need to be long, just a memo that would give the family closure in case we died on the battlefield. He was brief, just told us to write, address them, and then to hand the envelopes over to him. He'd make sure they made it to where they needed to go once you stepped on a mine, got shot by a friend, or were blown apart by a rocket-propelled grenade (RPG). Eighteen-year-old Marines had to drop their superman acts and face the truth of war—people die. As if a letter was going to make anyone feel better. We were left to ponder our young lives, to sum up our thoughts

16

on notebook paper, then seal it in an envelope. No stamp required. The government would pay for that.

The death letter speech was finished. Only a few minutes long, yet it lingered like a hangover. Grabbed the platoon by the balls. Yanked the short and curlies. The junior Marines weren't as good as the more seasoned men at suppressing their feelings, and I could tell they were rattled. A year ago, the hardest decision some of those guys had ever made was what color tuxedo they were going to wear to their senior proms. Now, instead of running around the tent playing grab-ass with each other, like they usually did, the young Marines were sitting on top of their dusty packs, eulogizing themselves. Most likely, they were writing the same type of macho bullshit that I wrote, trying to sound tough with their words in case words were all that made it home.

Kipper sat down beside me. He motioned for me to take off the headphones. I put my middle finger in his face. He pulled on the cord.

"What?" I said.

"I need to talk to you. Got a favor to ask."

His flak jacket was slung over his arm. He reached inside its front pocket, pulled out a can of chewing tobacco. He packed a wad into his mouth, licked the residue from his fingers, and wiped them across one of his black boot socks.

"Can't squeeze into your flak jacket?" I asked.

He didn't reply, which was uncommon. Any other time, he would have fired back with a sarcastic quip. Kipper was the king of quick comebacks, had a toolbox full of outlandish sayings. His silence made it obvious that he really wanted to talk about something and whatever was bothering him had nothing to do with the size of his flak jacket.

"Okay," I said. "What is it?"

"I need you to do something for me if . . ." He stopped, checked our surroundings to make sure nobody else in the tent was listening in on our conversation.

"*If* what?" I asked prematurely, not thinking about what "if" had come to mean to all of us.

"I have a bad feeling about all of this. A *really* bad feeling. I don't think I'm going to make it through." He glanced away again. "Look, before we left California, I wrote a letter for my wife. The kind the first sergeant was talking about. It's in the back of my flak jacket, sealed in a sandwich bag. I need you to make sure she gets it if something happens to me. It has to come from a friend: Brannon, Paxson, or you. Not the first sergeant or anyone else. Okay?"

"Sure, but can I stick it to her while I'm there?"

I had a will and several power of attorney forms filled out, signed, and notarized. I'd written my blood type in big, black letters on the top edges of both of my desert boots just in case something happened, and I could fully visualize a burial detail of Marines folding the American flag at my funeral as a lone bugler played taps. I thought I had prepared for everything, had mentally explored every possible situation. Yet I wasn't quite ready for what Kipper had asked me to do. It had been different coming from the first sergeant. Those are the kinds of things first sergeants were supposed to say, not your buddies. Kipper and I had known each other for so long that we couldn't remember a time when we hadn't known each other. We'd gotten drunk together more times than either of us could count. I'd laughed as he puked a combination of blood and tequila onto his chest the night of his twenty-first birthday four years earlier; had been a member of the sword detail at his wedding just a few months before we knew about Iraq. We'd trained together and fought in bars together, but never before thought we might die together.

Thinking about death, in private, was one thing, but having it verbalized was an entirely different matter. Sure, we all knew our profession and location made the probability of getting wasted rather high (and likely), but nobody talked about dying, ever. Most of us tried to ignore death, hoped it would go away or not happen or that if it did happen, it would happen so fast that we wouldn't realize it was happening. The cliché "He never knew what hit him" sounded all right to me.

Kipper left the tent. I leaned against a tent pole, placed my green notebook on my knees, and worked a pen across a blank page in the back. The front pages were filling up fast with the names of cities I couldn't spell, lists of missing gear, boot sizes for Marines who needed new boots, ammo counts, grid coordinates to places we might never go, passwords and challenge words, radio frequencies we didn't use, and time hacks we had to make. The back pages, however, belonged to me. Occasionally I would stop writing to watch the never-ending dominoes game a group of senior Staff NCOs played within spitting distance of my living area.

"Whatcha writing?" asked Gunny after he'd slapped a double five down and yelled at the Master Sergeant sitting across from him.

"Nothing really," I replied.

"A death letter?"

"No, Gunny. Just a letter home."

I wasn't writing home. I wasn't writing a death letter, either. I was writing a death journal, a piece of fiction meant for my family and my fiancée, Sara. Something they'd receive along with the rest of my belongings after I was killed in combat; something that told them I was courageous, unafraid, and ready to die.

I'd written as a warrior, masked any true feelings, and put down what I had wanted to believe, wanted others to believe. The company first sergeant told us to write down the truth, give it to him, and he'd mail it home. However, I lied, packed it away, and carried it with me.

2

I'LL BEAT THE FUCK out of you if you don't shut your goddamn mouth." The words erupted from my mouth, darted toward Sara like a cluster of heat-seeking missiles. Sergeant Van Winkle had surfaced. He pushed me out of the driver's seat and into the dark carport. Wearing a pair of sweat-stained cammies and tan combat boots with "O POS" stenciled across the top of them, he was poised to strike again. Ready to inject another dose of venom into his prey. I watched from afar, waited for sanity to return.

Silence. The bombed-out look on Sara's face said it all. I'd let a simple argument escalate into a nightmare, proven to her what she feared most: Her future husband was an IED (improvised explosive device), left roadside in Iraq, and anything was possible once he exploded. Maybe it wouldn't have been so bad if I hadn't meant what I'd said. But I had, every disgusting word, and I could tell she knew.

I wasn't able to hold back. Something primordial surged through my body and took over. The feeling coursed through my veins, possessed me. Tracer rounds were zipping overhead again. So I squeezed the trigger and fired rounds downrange. Unfortunately, just like bullets, you can never get words back once they have been sent out into the world.

For better or worse, always faithful, to have and to hold . . .

Sara leaned away from me, pressed her back against the car door and wouldn't take her eyes off of me. She searched out the door handle. Sergeant Van Winkle stepped out of the Jeep Cherokee, headed back to Iraq. The rumbling of his AAV rattled windows as it tore through my neighbors' yards, kicking up chunks of sod. Exhaust fumes poured from the top of the vehicle and made my eyes tear up, but only slightly. Sara went inside, leaving me to fester in my filth.

I was violent before I went to Iraq, yes, but never to Sara. Being a Marine, especially in a combat MOS, required a certain level of violence. Sara was fully aware of all of that. We'd been together for four years, met when I was a lance corporal, and she had witnessed my violent tendencies on numerous occasions, watched Kipper, Paxson, and me win a barroom brawl against a squad of Army guys at, of all places, Have A Nice Day Café in Norfolk. A dropkick executed in front of the police led to handcuffs and a three-hour ride in the shore patrol's paddy wagon. But that, for the most part, was controlled violence—we were responding to an attack, eliminating the threat.

A good Marine, one who follows what he's been taught, doesn't use unnecessary force and fights for people who can't fight for themselves. A good Marine doesn't take pleasure in violence and is able to control his emotions. Never would I have dreamt of threatening Sara in any way. Punch a wall, yes, but *never* yell or threaten her. Never. She wouldn't have put up with that type of behavior.

I wasn't at a crossroads. I'd passed through that checkpoint and was already halfway down the wrong road. What would be next? The thought scared me. "Fuck!" I yelled at the steering wheel. "What the fuck is wrong with me?"

Sara's long, blond hair spilled over the side of the couch. I leaned down, kissed the top of her head, tried to wish away the pain I had been causing her. She looked so peaceful, her slender body curled up on the couch, but I knew better. Sara had come to know grief well. During my deployment to Iraq, each time reports of another unidentified casualty had surfaced, she waited and prayed and hoped. When a van with government plates drove by her parents' house, she was almost certain of its mission. Even though girlfriends didn't rate a Casualty Call, she followed the van around the central Phoenix neighborhood, waited for it to pull into her driveway. If they had stopped, the uniformed men would've walked to the door carrying a flag or whatever it is they take when they go to inform a family that their loved one had just been wasted "on behalf of a grateful nation." And when they didn't stop at the house, she went home and cried at the thought that it might come back any day, if not to her parents' house, where she stayed while I was in Iraq, then to my mom's house in Virginia Beach, or to my hometown of Ocoee, Florida, to inform my dad.

After enduring the war, she must've thought everything was over, that things would be okay and we would settle down and move forward with our lives together. She'd been supportive even though I never told her anything about my combat tour in Iraq. But nothing had ended and there she was on the couch, in the position she had grown to know so well, once again sleeping away pain caused by me. The casualties kept accumulating.

Sure, I was happy being unhappy, but Sara didn't deserve that kind of treatment. Maniacal outbursts had become commonplace, but I had raised the bar, taken the craziness to another level by directing the anger toward her. Imploding was one thing, exploding was another.

A strong, self-reliant person like Sara didn't have to stay around. All she had to do was take off her engagement ring and be done with me, forever. Cut her losses and carry on. She could've forgotten about all of the madness, found somebody with fewer issues. She probably should have.

3

THERE IT WAS: ALL six stories of the hospital, staring at me, daring me to park my vehicle and venture into its belly. Palm trees and manicured lawns made Phoenix's Carl T. Hayden Veterans Administration Medical Center seem almost inviting. Apparently others got the same vibe from the landscaping because a dozen or so veterans, most of them clutching tallboys wrapped in brown paper bags, were crouched against the outside walls, enjoying what little shade they could find before the Department of Defense cops caught up with them and shooed them off the property. Clearly, the men were only trying to keep out of the sun's reach, and the inferno it had created, before being forced into the "real world" and back onto the streets they'd come from. The VA hospital looked more like a homeless shelter than a hospital. Platoons of homeless vets hovered around the medical center campus— an urban oasis for the neglected vets of Phoenix. I didn't know whether to be sad or disgusted or both.

A chubby, middle-aged man riding around the hospital's perimeter in an electric wheelchair didn't look homeless, but his presence was just as disturbing. A tattered American flag flapped from the back of his scooter as he patrolled the corner of the palm-lined street, waving his sign at passing cars. I stood in the parking lot, watched him scoot along Indian School Road, and tried to make sense of the WELCOME TO AUSCHWITZ sign his pudgy hands were wrapped around. Comparing the hospital to a concentration camp that shoved innocent people into ovens was a bit much, I thought, and probably in poor taste, but the government had ticked him off enough to make the comparison.

It was hard to believe a place like the VA had the ability to evoke such negative feelings in a veteran or that a single site could be teeming with so many homeless. If those were the "normal" patients, I couldn't wait to see what the mental health clinic had lingering in its halls.

I took a seat in a blue floral-pattern chair, which was probably bolted to the floor, and picked up an outdated magazine from the side table. I rubbed my eyes, looked over the top of the magazine. Nope, I wasn't hallucinating. The man sitting across from me did have on a floppy, pink sun hat, a *Support the Troops* T-shirt, and a pair of thick-rimmed Jackie O sunglasses. His flimsy white shirt was nearly translucent, revealing a training bra of some sort. There was a time when things must've been different for him, a time before he went around half cross-dressed. I tried to imagine him with a high and tight haircut, spit-shined boots, and a starched uniform with crisp creases. Anywhere else and I might have found it funny.

These are my people, I thought. Pissed-off and unstable veterans. Things sure had changed in a hurry.

Twelve months prior, I'd been darting around Iraq in charge of Marines and a section of AAVs. We were blowing stuff up, moving house to house, and securing neighborhoods. A mere year later, I was in the crazy-man clinic, seated across from a cross-dresser in a VA mental health clinic and, worst of all, probably only a few degrees saner. Sitting there seemed like a dream, so far away from anything that I had been, that I had ever planned on becoming. Losing control of my mind had never been a part of my plans.

My thoughts drifted in and out of the present, jumped between various places and events. I was at the VA hospital, but also in a Virginia Beach hotel room my first night home, and somewhere in Iraq. Just another day of time travel. I told myself to concentrate, think about the present, live. Don't look for a meaning in all of the madness. But there was no subduing it: The past wanted the present.

A collective moan rumbled through the cabin when the plane flew over Virginia. Marines pressed their faces against the portholes, tried to locate places they were familiar with.

"This is some stupid shit," Sterlachini said. "Do you see it? Huh, Van Winkle? You see what is below us? What genius decided it would be a good idea to fly us right over our homes and drop us off two thousand miles away?"

"Somebody call the Wambulance," I said. "Staff Sergeant has a case of vaginitis."

It was pretty easy for me to poke fun since I knew I wouldn't have to stay in California for too long, wouldn't demobilize with the reservists. The active-duty Marines would get a rental car and romp around Southern California while the rest of the company sat through demobilization classes and endured medical examinations. We'd drink beer and visit casinos. We'd go to the beach and eat burritos at Colimas in Oceanside.

Two days later. The active-duty Marines boarded a plane in San Diego. As a part of the advance party, we were on our way home while the rest of the company waited at Camp Pendleton. The six of us were about to meet up with our families for the first time in six months, then head our separate ways. We'd go home and take showers by ourselves: no cock-and-balls swinging within eyesight. Nobody throwing dice—and yelling "Snake Eyes bitch"—when we slept. No more late-night wake-ups by lance corporals who had misplaced their weapons or slept through fire watch. No more desert cammies or pop shots or patrolling. There wasn't any reason to be unhappy.

Gunny Rines ordered four cans of Bud Light from the

flight attendant. "Welcome home," she said as she passed out the beer. Kemling, Bailey, Gunny Rines, and I held our cans in the air. We toasted the war dead, finished the cans in one go. "More beer," Kemling said.

The plane pulled into the terminal. We remained in our seats and let the civilians disembark first.

I waited at the end of the ramp for everybody to assemble. All present and accounted for, forward march. It was a scary feeling. Even though we had been granted liberty for thirty-six hours when we arrived in California, that day was the first time I'd be around civilians sober, or without the remnants of that day-and-a-half-long drinking binge that almost killed me—and if it weren't for Gunny Rines saving my tail, I probably would've died in some gutter within the first few hours of my return. We were ghosts in California anyway, just another group of jarheads rolling through bars, getting drunk, and talking shit.

"Is it too late to turn back?" I asked the group.

"I know what you mean," answered Rines.

Bailey and Beck must have felt differently. While the rest of us marched shoulder to shoulder down the terminal, the two of them had sprinted ahead of us and were already embracing their wives.

It *was* too late to turn back. The families had already caught a glimpse of us and were howling like a pack of hyenas in heat. Within range of the shrieking crowd, within view of the homemade welcome home signs and crying women, I started to feel queasy. A spring opened up in my palms, sending rivers of sweat down my fingertips. What would I say? What could I say?

Turn back. Turn back. Turn back.

Only a handful of people had gathered in the Norfolk International Airport to welcome us home; no band, no parade, no ticker tape like the Desert Storm veterans had been subjected to—nothing like I had imagined, but I was thankful for the lackluster greeting. I wanted to see my family, but didn't want to leave the other guys. The people waiting for us were strangers, even though I knew every last one of them.

Hugs from the civilians felt as foreign as walking around without a weapon. Sara wrapped her arms around my neck and squeezed. Her tear-soaked cheek dampened my collar. I looked beyond her, surveyed the passing crowds of people, sized each one up, and looked for anything out of place. Ten minutes of how-ya-doin's and high fives, then we collected our dusty, olive drab seabags and went our separate ways. That's it? I should've realized the anticlimactic return home would only foreshadow things to come, that nothing would ever again be what it seemed.

Sara and I went to a beachfront hotel. I soaked in a hot tub, tried to scrub Iraq from my body. We ate pizza and watched television until she fell asleep. Then, for the first time in six months, I was completely on my own.

From the balcony of my hotel room, I watched the waves rise and fall. The Atlantic Ocean pulsed, thrusting its salt water onto the beach, giving and taking a little of the shore each time. Spotlights on the hotel's roof pointed down toward the water, made the whitecaps glow. The dream of home that had bounced around my head for so long was reality. But despite the ocean's cooing, happiness eluded me. I missed my sleeping bag and the Marines I'd just left. I wondered what Kipper, Paxson, and the rest of the guys were doing, if they were awake, thinking about the war, too.

The ocean continued to sing its lullaby. It beckoned me to calm down and enjoy what was before me. A salty breeze whipped into the room. Mylar balloons bounced against the ceiling. Sara slept. As I looked at her nestled beneath the covers, it occurred to me that we didn't really know each other anymore. It wasn't her fault; I didn't know myself anymore either. So much had changed in the short time I was gone. I used to be able to tell her everything, but that was no longer possible. I didn't want to talk about the war, not with her, not with anyone else who hadn't been there. There was too much to explain. The stories were too complex.

I spat over the balcony. The stream floated in the wind before landing on the white slab of concrete below. So many nights I had sprawled out on top of my AAV and stared into the sky, watching the stars, anticipating that one moment I'd be away from the carnage. The first night in Baghdad I watched red tracer rounds and rockets sail through the night sky. Bombs brought fire to the ground, made buildings submit to their force. Fire fluttered through the darkness from various sections of the city. Explosions rattled the earth. That destruction was the most beautiful thing I'd ever seen. Clusters of stars winked through the madness, as bright as ever, like a bottle of glitter dumped from heaven. I wrote a letter to Sara about the Baghdad stars, how bright and clear they were, how they seemed to be within arm's reach. The same stars looked much different from the balcony, so far away and dull.

Teeter-tottering on the balcony's railing, I felt my lifelong fear of heights cease for a moment. So I draped the rest of my body over the waist-high metal railing and stared up at the pale stars. This is what you wanted, I thought. Here it is, the moment you couldn't wait for, surrounded by the things you only hoped to see again. I had everything—all my fingers and toes, Sara, a bucket load of war stories (real and imagined), and full access to a first-rate, porcelain toilet. Why did I want more and what exactly was it that I wanted? There were more questions than answers. More confusion than clarity.

I felt lost without my sidekick Kipper to talk with; no Gunny Yates, no Gunny Rines, no Staff Sergeant Paxson, or Sergeant Bailey. Nobody within miles who had a clue; nobody who even knew where Nasiriyah or Al Kut was located. So, I thought, this is the life of a combat vet?

My body ached from the lack of sleep. I'd only managed to squeeze in a few hours' worth of naps between eating splurges and television watching those first few days. Then, back to work—back to the unit, back to see the Marines. I swerved in and out of traffic, honked my horn liberally, looked for a reason to start a fight or run someone off the road. I wasn't afraid of crashing or becoming a road-rage casualty. None of that mattered. I welcomed trouble, wanted it.

Blue lights reflected in my rearview mirror. I pulled over, watched a Department of Defense police officer swagger up to my window. He tapped on the glass. I rolled it down halfway, expecting he'd make me endure a sobriety test once he saw my bloodshot eyes and sleepless condition.

"Do you know why I pulled you over?" he asked. I intended to go through the motions and play along but couldn't. What was he going to do, shave my head and send me to Iraq? My mouth overruled what little sense I had and took charge of the situation.

"'Cause you wanted to say hi." He thumped his ticket book. "I don't have time to play your guessing games. How about you give me a ticket so I can get to work."

"Sir—"

"Are you going to give me a ticket or not? If not, I'm leaving."

I don't know where the words came from; they just spewed from my mouth without the first thought of the consequences. It was pure Gunny Yates. The officer began to lecture me but I cut him off.

"I really don't have time for this. So, give me a ticket or let me go. Either way, make it quick. Gunny is going to have my ass if I'm late for work." A Marine MP would have had me hog-tied already.

"Late for work? What do you think your gunnery sergeant

will say when he has to pick you up from the brig?" That slowed my roll a bit.

"Sir," I said, using an amicable tone, "I'm a little irritable right now. I just got back from Iraq and haven't slept much."

I was lucky and got off with a warning. The officer let me go, only telling me I needed to slow down before someone got hurt and that maybe I should rethink how I spoke to police officers.

At work, I went straight to Gunny's office, took a seat in front of his desk beneath the framed Smokey Bear cover he had hanging on the wall, and explained what had happened with the DoD cop. While Gunny should've chewed my ass out for such an act, he didn't. Instead, he seemed proud of what he had helped to create and sent me away without any type of reprimand, just told me I needed to calm down and go with the flow. I went to my office and fell asleep.

Three days later, the reservists flew home. Gunny, Bailey, and I donned our desert cammies for the reservists' homecoming and prepared to pick them up from the airport.

Staff Sergeant Braudis, our active-duty armorer, issued an M16 and sixty rounds of 5.56 to me. I slid the rounds into magazines, individually, without using a speed loader, savoring each round as it clicked into place. Adoring their brass casings and green tips. The "Guardian Angel" detail provided the opportunity to carry a loaded weapon again. My job: ensure that nobody tried to harm the Marines. Ride in a van, scan the tree lines, the rooftops, look for anything out of place.

Hundreds of family members crowded the inside of the

compound. They'd plastered signs along the brick buildings and on the chain-link fencing. Women wore short skirts and brightly colored blouses, had manicured fingernails and toe-nails and fancy hairdos. The Guardian Angel detail unloaded first, then the rest of the Marines.

Gunny Donahoo had bets on which of the Marines would cry. He even had it divided into levels of crying, from a few teardrops to straight-out bawling. I saw him looking into the crowd for a winner. Still no ticker tape, band, or parade. I moved away from the crowd, patrolled the perimeter, and got lost in my patrol—my last patrol. I watched the cars drive down the road and waited for someone to make a wrong move and try to plow through the gates. I wanted to fire a weapon one last time, hear brass casings hitting pavement. I wanted more action.

Walking the perimeter with a rifle gave me a feeling of sat-isfaction and purpose. It was almost euphoric. I liked the way the M16's ribbed, fiberglass hand guards felt in my left hand; the way the nylon sling coiled around my forearm; how the buttstock nestled into my underarm; and the feeling of the cold metal against my right index finger—which was straight and off the trigger—as I stroked the lower receiver of the weapon. I liked having rules of engagement again and author-ization to use deadly force, if needed. I liked the way my boots squished in the thick green grass as I moved through the adja-cent field, looking for trouble, protecting the Marines. The balcony seemed light-years away. We were all back together and I had a loaded weapon. No feelings of loneliness or confusion, not with a weapon in my hand and Marines to back me up.

Two weeks later, I was on terminal leave, out of the Corps and away from the rifle and Marines—on a different balcony, overlooking my future, watching the waves crash into the rocky shore below.

"Iraq." A squeaky voice brought my thoughts back to the present, back to the gloom of the waiting room. "I'd have rather been there," the voice continued. I looked over at the dark-haired woman seated a few chairs to my right. She had started her session early and was telling her life story to the man sitting next to her, but loud enough for the entire clinic to hear. She had convinced herself that she had been stationed at the roughest place in the world and was saying something about an Air Force base in Germany. According to her, people were getting their heads lopped off daily there. If I was crazy, she was insane. She got louder, raised her arms in the air like she was awarding field goals to a ghost football team. Her greasy black hair swung from side to side with each motion of her fidgety hands, swished across the top of a faux leather fighter pilot jacket that had an array of patriotic buttons (with slogans like "These Colors Don't Run" and "God Bless America") dotted across it. I raised a magazine in front of my face and stared into it.

The clinic continued to fill with veterans of varying degrees of mental stability, but nobody else quite as crazy as the

Air Force chick or the cross-dresser showed up. A clean-shaven guy in his midtwenties took a seat a few rows over from me. It appeared that he had recently been discharged from the military and had been relegated to waiting for his few minutes with a doctor, who would no doubt hand over a prescription for something that would make everything better again. A small pin protruded from the side of his baseball cap: a golden George Washington shrouded in purple. I wanted to ask the guy where he'd served, see if we'd chewed the same dirt or passed each other at some point in Iraq. He may have lived at the same camp in Baghdad or driven through Hillah as my unit secured the road. I didn't say anything, though, kept listening to the crazy girl and ignored the possibility of any corresponding past.

Maybe the guy in the floppy pink hat had a Purple Heart, too, stuffed away in a drawer beneath his training bras. Maybe he'd earned the Medal of Honor at Hue City for pulling an entire platoon of injured Marines from a pile of rubble. Something had driven him over the edge. Did he have nightmares? Was he called a baby killer when he came home? Did anyone care that he made it home? I was afraid I would find myself in the same position, not wearing a training bra, but hopelessly lost in a battle of the past: still fighting through the desert, ducking rounds, and shooting ghosts.

A nurse wobbled out from behind a Wizard of Oz curtain and waved me into her office, away from my screwball counterparts. There were no pleasantries exchanged. She didn't offer a seat or even make eye contact. I wondered if I'd forgotten to put deodorant on or if there was something hanging out of my nose. I wiped my face and snuck a sniff. Nothing.

"You're an Iraq vet?"

'Yes, ma'am. I—"

"Do you feel like hurting yourself?"

"No."

"Do you feel like hurting anyone else?"

"When I'm driving I want to run people over. I want to run other cars off the road when they piss me off."

"That's normal."

That's fucking normal? Jesus Christ, where? Somalia?

According to the certificate she had strategically placed on her wall in front of where she seated her patients, she'd been an officer in the Army medical corps. I wasn't impressed but expected that a fellow veteran would be somewhat helpful, maybe even a little caring. Instead, I received drive-through window service. I'm not sure how far she thought she was going to get with her condescending, elitist attitude, because the game she was trying to play didn't appeal to me. We weren't in the service anymore. I didn't have to salute her, didn't have to call her ma'am, and certainly didn't have to kiss her ass because she'd been a commissioned officer in the U.S. Army. I could've told her to pull the stick out of her ass and get over herself. If there was going to be any ass kissing, the nurse should've been kissing mine My craziness kept her in business. I didn't say anything. Sergeant Van Winkle stayed in the barracks.

"Post-traumatic stress disorder," she said.

"Huh?" I replied.

I heard what she'd said, but it didn't quite register. There had to be some mistake. Surely the nurse wasn't suggesting that *I* had PTSD. She had to be talking about somebody else. I'd been a sergeant of Marines. I wasn't moping around or crying over the stuff I'd done. Sure, there were the nightmares, insomnia, and heavy drinking, but PTSD? C'mon: I wanted to hurt *other* people.

There is a stigma attached to that acronym, one I didn't want to be associated with. I thought of it as a form of castration, a medical term for nonhacker. I'd gone to the clinic to find a way to control the rage that was burning inside of me, to find ways to deal with the anger before I did anything stupid or drank myself out of a marriage. The diagnosis only made me angrier. I didn't think I was *that* crazy.

I clutched the arms of the chair. Sweat dripped from my palms, created a pool on the tiled floor below. The diagnosis wasn't what I'd expected, not even close. I could handle being called an asshole or crazy, but not being called a nonhacker. What would Gunny think if he found out about this? How could I look any of the Marines in the face knowing a VA nurse claimed I had PTSD?

There wasn't enough time to get into the specifics or to argue for a new diagnosis. I was going to have those four miserable letters etched into my permanent records whether I wanted them in there or not. PTSD. And that was it: She stood up and pointed me on my way. I left the clinic with a prescription for antidepressants I had no intention of taking and an appointment four weeks later for an initial consultation with a doctor. Nothing solved, just diagnosed and set free angrier than I'd been when I'd arrived. I could only hope for a more positive experience with the doctor. He'd be better. He had to be.

The cast of characters I had kept company with in the waiting room had disappeared into the system, eaten up by the big VA machine. A fresh batch of mentally impaired vets had taken their place on the bureaucratic merry-go-round, waiting to be herded into holding cells for their five-minute interrogations and rations of feel-better pills.

The walk down the hallway seemed much longer. The hall seemed bigger. Had the place doubled in size or had I gotten smaller? While things weren't right before, at that moment everything was completely out of whack. I'd had to talk myself into going to the clinic in the first place, had to tell myself it was all right to seek treatment. In return, I'd been treated like a second-class citizen and told that I was worse than I ever could have imagined.

On the way home, a middle-aged man in the median tried to get my attention. It was over a hundred degrees outside, but he was still patrolling the streets, looking to make a few bucks by scrubbing filth off of car windshields when they stopped at the light. He waved a bottle of Windex at me. Shook his washrag in the air. I turned up the radio and looked away. No time for bums. Even though I refused to make eye contact or acknowledge he existed, he kept walking toward my vehicle. He didn't seem *too* crazy, but he was definitely on a mission of some sort. A mission I didn't want any part of.

I slid my right hand between the seat and center console, unsheathed a Marine Corps–issued KA-Bar fighting knife. Staff Sergeant Braudis had once showed me how to get the blade sharp enough to cut through skin without having to apply much pressure, and its seven-inch blade was just as sharp as it had ever been. I'd slice the bum open if he gave me any trouble, let his blood ooze onto the asphalt.

The man stopped in front of my vehicle. He laughed when I revved the engine, then bent down and washed the mixture of smashed bugs and dried mud from the USMC license plate that was bolted onto the front of my Jeep. No doubt he was attempting to make the gold letters radiate from the red background. He stood up, pulled his heels together, and saluted the license plate, then me. It was a perfectly executed salute: right hand raised smartly with his fingers and thumb extended and joined, palm turned slightly. A platoon of goose bumps paraded up my arms. I slid the KA-Bar back into its worn leather sheathe, rolled down the window, and extended my right hand to him. A USMC tattoo inked into his right biceps showed itself when he reached for my hand.

"No charge," he said. "Semper Fi, Marine."

"Always," I replied.

I left the windows down for the rest of the ride home. It felt like I was riding around in an AAV again. The desert air circulated through my vehicle, blew the hair-dryer heat into my face. I'd given the window-washing Marine a few bucks before the light turned green. He said he didn't want it, but I insisted. I felt it was the least I could do for a fellow veteran. I didn't know what had caused his hard times or led him to the streets, but none of that mattered. I'd been treated like a bum at the VA and didn't like the feeling, and didn't want any other Marine to have to feel that way, especially not because of me.

Instead of going straight home, I stopped at a Mexican restaurant that was a few blocks away from my house. A salt-rimmed glass and pitcher of margaritas on the rocks were waiting for me. The waitress took the menu off the table. Pictures from Iraq filled the television screen. I didn't need the TV to remind me; I had pictures of my own drifting through my head. I downed the first glass, poured another.

It could've been worse: I left Iraq with all the body parts I'd shipped out with and my unit made it home in one piece. So why was my life so messed up? Why was there so much chaos in my head? Did I participate in enough combat to have PTSD? See enough death? Kill enough people?

The more I drank, the more I remembered. The more I remembered, the more I tried to forget. I had another pitcher and two bottles of beer. Four more weeks, I thought. Hang in there for another four weeks.

4

THE HOURS BLURRED INTO days, the days into weeks. I was marking time, stuck in the past. That first visit to the crazy-man clinic seemed like it had happened several years prior rather than a couple of weeks.

Living off savings, student loans, and thousand-dollar-a-month GI Bill payments, I didn't have to work while attending college. Sara waited tables at her grandfather's restaurant, went to school, and interned for her teaching degree. When she was home, I was usually asleep. The combination must've made life, for her, bearable.

All the free time left too much time for drinking and remembering. School, compared to the Marine Corps, was easy, didn't take a whole lot of effort. While a piss-poor term paper might have been painful for the professor who was forced to read it, nobody was going to die if I misinterpreted Donne.

I poured half a glass of rum, topped it off with a splash of Coke, and then took the bottle into my computer room. My yellow Lab followed. She nuzzled her head against my leg. I rubbed her ear, stared at a wooden box that held all the mementos I'd brought back from Iraq. All the physical evidence from my desert adventure was crammed into the box: pictures from disposable cameras; a wad of dinars with Saddam's picture plastered across the fronts; a Republican Guard beret I found lying on the ground in Baghdad; a small tricolor Iraqi flag; and my death journal. I dropped an ice cube for the dog and then retrieved the box.

Iraqi sand still covered the war trophies. Grime was jammed and pressed into the objects' crevices and cracks. The box released the land when I opened it, sending a small sandstorm toward my face. I closed my eyes, inhaled the particles. A kaleidoscope of sights overwhelmed me. Images swirled out of order, meshing the whole war experience into one big slide show: Hillah, Shatra, Baghdad, Kut, Diwiniyah, Kuwait, Nasiriyah, and home were a jumble of pictures in my head. I couldn't distinguish what had happened in each place. The stories didn't fit either, and I knew there were places and events I had been neglecting or had completely forgotten. I reached over and turned the radio up, poured another drink.

My yellow Lab bolted from the room, ran down the hall, and started barking at the front door. I grabbed a 20-gauge shotgun from the closet, stuffed my front pockets full of shells, and went to investigate. With a little luck, I would get the chance to load a burglar's face full of birdshot.

Boots clunked against the tiled floor, echoed through the hallway. I pointed the shotgun barrel toward the front door. Kipper rushed ahead. Paxson coughed from the dirt that had been kicked up by the sudden movement. I looked back.

"Pax," I whispered. "What are you and Kipper doing here?"

"You didn't think we'd let you go alone, did you?"

"Go where?" I asked.

"That's up to you. We're just along for the ride. But it looks like you're taking us somewhere, and wherever the fuck it is, we'd better get moving. Gunny is waiting," he said.

Three AAVs were staged and waiting for us. We each climbed into a different vehicle. Kipper and Paxson's vehicles tore off in separate directions, back to their sections. I charged the .50 caliber machine gun and then spun the turret around. Gunny Yates radioed over to me.

"Stinky, this is Buckeye."

"This is Stinky," I said. "Send it."

"Prepare to move out."

We moved through the desert, to a city that sat somewhere between Nasiriyah and Baghdad. It had a name, I am sure, but to us it was just a grid coordinate, a spot on the map, another roadblock on our journey to Baghdad. Our company stopped on a stretch of hardball road that led into the city and waited for the CO to give us the word to move in. Operations flowed like a symphony, and we were preparing for the unseen conductor to wave his baton so we could raise our instruments and play our part.

The city looked like it was either sinking into the sand or had recently risen from it. Fronded vegetation surrounded a series of irrigation canals that cut through the seemingly endless desert and divided the city into two halves.

Move out. The AAVs dispersed. Each section took a different sector of the city. Lance Corporal Bello stopped our AAV in the middle of town and lowered the ramp. The grunts unloaded, walked by an antiaircraft gun, through a set of steel gates and into the courtyard of an abandoned elementary school. Unfired shells encircled the Soviet-made weapon, which pointed into the cloudless blue sky. All clear. We moved forward, cleared the rest of the homes on the near side of the canal.

The grunts crossed the canal over a path of raised earth that wasn't wide enough for our vehicles. Bello drove the AAV to the canal's edge, stopped in front of a single-level home, and waited. Half the squad of grunts went inside while the other half walked around the building. Still eager to shoot something, anything, I pressed a pair of binoculars to my eyes and looked for a target to destroy.

Trackers in another section claimed to have spotted an Iraqi ambulance or car moving through the streets. It was one or the other, maybe both. But since eyewitness accounts were often as sketchy as Big Foot sightings, you could never be too sure of what you were about to face. All you could do was adhere to the rules of engagement and hope for a "clean shoot" that didn't involve civilians.

Two Cobra helicopters buzzed overhead. They swooped in low, hovered above the warehouse complex to my left. The lead Cobra opened fire, caused chunks of steel to rip away from the building. Not three seconds later, the second gunship released a portion of its arsenal.

"Sergeant, see anything?" Bello asked.

"Nope, you?"

"No, Sergeant, nothing."

I lowered the binoculars and faced the driver's station. His eyes were fixed on me like he could magically see through my binoculars as well.

"Nothing, huh?"

"No, Sergeant."

"Because you're staring at me. Turn around," I said.

The grunts watched over the occupants of the home they were searching. They had about twenty women and children sitting cross-legged in front of the house. No threat. I moved my binoculars between the helicopters and house, still looking for the ghost vehicle that was reportedly driving through the city.

A sharp, raspy voice cut through the speakers in my comm helmet, into my ears. It was Gunny Yates. He'd found a safe route across the canal, something our AAVs could easily pass. He guided me to the area. I signaled my other vehicles. We moved in a column past the school to another stretch of the canal. The grunts moved deeper into the city, away from the firepower the AAVs offered. One by one, each AAV crossed the canal.

We drove through the narrow streets unafraid, barely cautious. We'd only been in Iraq for a week but already felt somewhat seasoned. The routine had basically been the same: Go to a city with a name we couldn't pronounce and let the grunts toss homes while the AAVs kept watch. Every once in a while, to make things a little more exciting, Bello would take charge of the turret and Lance Corporal Meyers, our rear crewman-section mechanic would drive, so I could patrol on the ground with the grunts. Although Second Lieutenant Frank, the grunts' platoon commander, often extended the invitation, I seldom took it. My place was in the turret of an AAV.

Gunny Yates, on the other hand, was all over the country. He headed wherever he thought he would get the most action. Gunny had to be in the middle of everything. Dying didn't scare him. However, Gunny Yates planned on taking out as many enemy combatants as he could before they got him. The way Gunny saw it, the more enemy he could kill, the better, because each warm body he dropped meant one less person with the ability to harm his Marines.

A family of four stood outside their busted-up home and watched us while a squad of grunts searched the shack across the road.

"Can I throw candy down to them?" Bello asked.

"Don't waste anything good," I answered. Bello held up a pack of Charms. "Yeah, go ahead."

Bello tossed the Charms to a bearded man. He inspected the pack, unwrapped a few of the pieces and then passed the fruit-flavored candy out to his family, first to his barefooted girls who were wearing long dirty dresses, then his wife. A grin stretched across their faces. The father smiled as well and then waved. And for a brief moment, we weren't Marines or liberators: just humans interacting with other humans.

The rest of the city's residents stayed inside until they were roused and made to stand outside as the grunts tore through their homes. Many of the families appeared less than happy about being temporarily displaced, but the sight of our weapons kept them silent. We continued to clear the city for two or three more hours. House to house. The same routine over and over again. I knew our big fight had to be in there somewhere. I hoped it was. Nasiriyah had whetted my appetite a few days before, had me wanting more. I wanted to fire my weapon again, wanted to see a .50 caliber round rip through an enemy combatant. Up close, that is.

We crossed back over the canal and began our movement to the assembly area. The grunts went into another house. An irrigation system jetted from the canal into the yard. Another broke from it and flowed to the house across the road. The ditches made the whole area muddier than the rest of the city, but a thin layer of grass hid the depth. The grunts stormed into the house; two sheep trotted out.

Positioned between the two houses, my AAV was in a bad

position. A pissed-off Iraqi with a grudge could've lobbed a grenade into the troop compartment and made us that day's ten-second news blip: just a few more names scrolling across the bottom of the television screen. I ordered Bello to move the vehicle away from the area. The vehicle lunged forward. Stopped. Bello pivoted the AAV. Its tracks dug into the mud. The front of the vehicle lowered slightly.

"Goddamn it, Bello. Are we stuck?"

"No, Sergeant," he replied.

The grunts filed out of the house. Clearing homes was a tedious process and the heat had taken its toll on them. They were moving much slower than they had been earlier, weighed down by their sweat-drenched cammies and muddy boots. The Marines crossed a dirt field. Bello put the vehicle in gear. It rolled a foot ahead, then stopped. The engine continued to rev.

"Sergeant."

"What, Bello?" I knew what he was about to say but didn't want to believe it.

"Sergeant, we're stuck."

Bello climbed down from the driver's station and onto the muddy ground. I pulled myself out of the turret and made my descent. As soon as my boots hit the soggy deck, I charged and brought my face within inches of his.

"You've got to be kidding? What the fuck did I tell you?" It was a rhetorical question. I didn't want an answer. "Didn't I tell you not to get fucking stuck? And what'd you go and do. Full speed ahead into the deepest mud hole you could find."

Bello opened his mouth to give an explanation.

"Shut up. Shut your goddamn mouth."

But Bello wasn't the type of Marine you could scare with mere words. Nothing ever seemed to faze "Mellow Bello." He just stared back with an I-don't-give-a-shit look.

The few grunts that had stayed back with us hauled tail at the first sign of digging. And before I could say, "Where do you guys think you're going?" which wouldn't have done much good anyway since I wasn't in their chain of command, they were halfway across the empty field and caught up with the rest of their squad. Kicking in doors did seem like a better gig than slinging mud.

We were stationary, and alone, in a city we'd spent the day ransacking, just waiting for something bad to happen. I was embarrassed. The vehicle was stuck because of me. The embarrassment turned to anger. I often faked being angry in order to convey my message to junior Marines, but that time I was actually furious. I knew the situation we were in was my fault. It's always the leader's fault, but I deflected the blame. It became Bello's fault. I threw my helmet against vehicle. It bounced off the side and landed in the mud.

Bello took the fall for everything. He carried the weight of both of our mistakes. As if the stress of war wasn't enough, I stayed on his ass constantly. I had the authority to relieve my stress on him. He had no authority and was forced to take it. So I yelled at him when the vehicle got stuck even though I could've stopped it. Like a hurricane hitting the beach, I roared in his ear, battered his spirit.

I closed the gap between us, squeezed my hands into fists. We were close, close enough that I could feel the heat of his breath and probably could've held a piece of paper between our noses. I readied myself to punch him.

"Hold on, stop right there. I am pretty sure they didn't teach you that in the Martial Arts Instructor School or at Sergeants Course. What a shitbag! You can't go around punching your troops," Paxson said. My yellow Lab was still barking at the front door. "Well, go ahead and let's see how this plays out."

"No, I'm done," I said.

"If only it were that easy."

Bello didn't budge. He may have been a skinny guy, but he was a tough Marine. He'd take a punch, probably even throw one back at me. What did he have to lose anyway?

"Get the shovel and start digging."

"Aye, aye, Sergeant."

He climbed into the vehicle. I kicked the track.

"Bring the pickax, too," I yelled. "And a couple of canteens."

Digging the thick mud away from the rusty steel tracks was like spooning water out of the ocean. We weren't making any progress, just moving mud from one place to another. Sweat poured from our bodies. I handed Bello a canteen, told him to get into the driver's station and try to move the AAV forward. He put the vehicle in gear, pressed on the accelerator. The engine wailed, dug the AAV, and our morale, deeper into the ground.

There was nothing else we could do. We needed to get another vehicle to tie towropes up to so we could be pulled out before dark. The rest of the platoon was still in the process of clearing the city and couldn't be bothered. The mission would be accomplished with or without me and there was only one person available who could take care of the situation. As much as I dreaded doing it, I would have to call Gunny Yates for help.

I'd been easy on Bello compared to how Gunny would treat me if we caught him in a foul mood.

"Buckeye, this is Stinky."

"Send it."

Lucky for me, it sounded like Gunny was in a good mood. I tried to sugarcoat the situation, so the rest of the platoon wouldn't find out, but Gunny insisted on hearing it over the radio. The secret was out: Sergeant Van Winkle had gotten his vehicle stuck. I knew that by the time we met back up with the rest of the platoon, the lance corporal connection would have morphed the story into something bigger, would've twisted the entire event around so that it sounded like I had driven an AAV into one of the canals. Fucking lance corporals, I thought. We'll see how funny they think it is when I give them all fire watch.

Gunny's AAV stopped in front of ours, away from the mud. Gunny smirked at the sight of our mud-covered vehicle, which was leaning slightly to the right. Staff Sergeant Beck, Gunny Donahoo, and their two crewmen jumped out of the AAV. Three Staff NCOs meant three more people I'd have to take shit from. Gunny Donahoo would certainly pile it on.

"Goddamn, Stinky, I've never seen a vehicle stuck this bad," said Gunny Yates. Staff Sergeant Beck licked the end of an MRE spoon clean and then pointed at my vehicle with it. "Yeah, good one, Van Winkle."

Gunny Yates supervised the digging, making fun of me in the process. He guided the drivers. Back and forth, back and forth: The vehicles played tug-of-war with each other. More digging. We repeated the process several times, covering ourselves in muck. After thirty minutes of digging, yanking, and sweating, the mud released the vehicle. "That'll cost you a steak dinner," said Gunny Yates.

Both vehicles pulled away. Gunny and I stayed behind, walked around the area. We made our way toward the two muddy vehicles, which had been parked a few blocks ahead of us. Gunny spotted something moving in a small, V-shaped irrigation ditch.

"Enemy Iraqi frog!" he yelled.

He pulled his pistol from its holster, pointed it at the frog.

"You don't have the balls," I said.

Two shots. No more ribbit. No more frog.

"That'll be another steak dinner, Junior," he said.

The grunts cleared the city. I got stuck. Marine Air blew some stuff up. Gunny shot an unarmed frog. We'd made it through another day, which at any other time would've been pretty exciting. But the big fight never came, never showed up like we had hoped.

It was late in the afternoon and everyone was worn out by the time we got the two vehicles back to the assembly area in a clearing across from the city. Marines were eating chow, relaxing, and awaiting the word to move on to another position. I had taken off my boots and was getting ready to wipe my feet down with baby wipes when Kipper walked onboard. He plopped down on the center bench in the back of my vehicle. What he liked to call a "shit-eating grin" was plastered across his face. "Okay, go ahead and have your fun." I stood up and poked my head out of the vehicle, looked at the hasty checkpoint the grunts had erected by simply pulling a strand of concertina wire across the two-lane road.

"Decided to go mudding while the rest of us patrolled. Sounds like fun," he said.

"Loads."

"Was Gunny pissed?"

"No, but I owe him another steak dinner."

"How many does that make?"

"He said seven, but I think he squeezed a couple in on me."

Kipper pulled a can of chewing tobacco out of his cargo pocket.

"Want a pinch?" he asked.

"Yeah, could use one."

I took the can from him, opened it, and stuffed a large portion of the wintergreen-flavored tobacco between my lip and gum. Getting chew was the best thing that had happened all day. One-ounce cans of Kodiak or fresh Copenhagen were scarce and valuable. You could easily sell one for twenty dollars, sometimes much more.

"Where'd you get this?"

"Traded a grunt two packs of jalapeño cheese spread and a pound cake for it."

"Good deal."

Kipper grabbed the can from me, thumped it with his finger a few times, and then placed a pinch in his mouth. He only managed to get half of the tobacco in place. The rest of it blended in with his dirt-covered face. He ran his tongue around the edge of his mouth, and then spat a brown stream into the soft dirt.

"Vehicle incoming!" yelled a grunt.

I ran out of the vehicle barefooted and leapt down into the prone position behind one of the vehicle's steel tracks. I sighted in with my pistol, although I knew I wasn't in range. Only my head and arms extended past the front of the AAV. A white Nissan truck was barreling down the road, headed straight for the stretched coil of concertina wire. The small truck seemed to pick up speed the closer it got. A lance corporal with a SAW (squad automatic weapon) started sending rounds downrange; then every weapon in the area began to fire. Kipper draped his body halfway across my back, handed his M16 to me. I passed my pistol to him, pressed the butt of his rifle into my shoulder.

Here it is, our big fight, I thought. I knew the lone vehicle would penetrate our perimeter, opening the way for a slew of well-armed Saddam fedayeen.

We were well within the M16's maximum effective range of eight hundred meters for an area target. I steadied, aimed, scanned. They hadn't given us time to get nervous. No adrenaline flowed. I was on automatic pilot, going through the motions, ready to fight but ambivalent about the possibility of death, our deaths. Sight alignment, sight picture, breath control; like I'd learned on the Parris Island rifle range. It all seemed as natural as walking.

"They're shooting back," yelled a Marine a few yards behind us. My thumb clicked the rifle's selector lever off SAFE and onto SEMI.

An obscene pinball game broke out. Rounds bounced off our vehicles in the orgy of gunfire. An overeager Marine a few yards behind our position nearly scored a friendly fire kill: He pointed and shot, but the round ricocheted off the amtrac that was parked on our left flank. *Ding, ding, ding*—just a *ding* away from death. I'm sure they would've told my parents I was a hero.

The truck rolled across the concertina wire, veered down an embankment, and ploughed its front end into the ground. All the shooting stopped. In two minutes, we probably wasted more money in ammo than most countries have in their entire defense budget. No telling where half of those rounds eventually impacted, or what kind of damage they did to the city we had spent the day clearing. Certainly, some unsuspecting person had taken one to the head.

Holes dotted the truck. Pieces of its shattered windshield littered the ground. I jogged over to it through the dusty and hollow landscape that was as barren as the surface of the moon. A squad of grunts had already made it to the Nissan by the time I got there and were in the process of tossing two Iraqis onto the ground. The driver's limp body, filled with American lead, dropped into the dirt. The blood-drenched passenger writhed in pain, kicking his legs and arms around as a Navy corpsman attempted to patch the man's wounds. Marines searched the truck. Nothing.

We left the men in the dirt, went back to eating chow. Pieces of their clothes flapped in the wind. A white flag too late. Evidence of what a wrong turn could do when the U.S. Marines were present. Sorry for your luck, I thought.

I never quite cared they'd been shot. It just happened. I did, however, feel somewhat dissatisfied since I hadn't gotten the opportunity to fire my weapon. I wanted to shoot. I wanted to send a bullet into the windshield and pulverize both of them. But I didn't get the chance, and I was unhappy. Bullets were my drugs and I desperately needed a fix.

I was enjoying the great human trophy hunt and, looking back, it scares the hell out of me.

My dog stopped barking before I made it to the front door. It was still light outside and the carport was empty. Nobody was going to get shot. No urban firefight would take place in my neighborhood. I grabbed a beer from the refrigerator and went back to the office. Kipper was sitting there, thumbing through a picture album.

"Put the gun away before you do something stupid," he said.

"Like what?"

"Look around. There's an empty bottle of rum. It's the middle of the afternoon, you have the stereo cranked, your Iraq memorabilia flung around the room, and you're carrying a shotgun around the house. Sounds like a winning combination. Plus, what the fuck am I doing here?"

"Don't know. Sometimes you and Pax appear when I think about Iraq. It's not like I plan any of the shit."

"If you didn't drink so much you probably wouldn't see things. Try laying off the booze, bozo."

"Go to hell," I said.

"Lead the way, Sergeant."

Our convoy zigzagged further into the country, through thickets of date palms and stretches of desert. Greenery sprouted near rivers, cutting through the tan wastelands. Pillared mansions sprawled in the midst of rubble piles. The land seemed familiar. The dark-skinned people reminded me of the people I had learned about in my Sunday school lessons and in the Bible Boy Scout troop called the Royal Rangers. I had thought the Royal Rangers were a thing of the past, something I had been forced to do as a kid. Never did I think I would be a Royal Ranger again, in the land of the Bible, killing for peace.

What would Jesus do? Surely he'd grab an M16 and invade. Send in the Royal Rangers. Make sure they knew the books of the Bible, the names of the apostles, and then arm them. March the boys to Eden. Tell them to kill the people they studied.

We passed an Iraqi who was resting against the steering wheel of an open-topped military truck. From the neck up he appeared alive: an intact beard and untouched face. But below the face and scraggly beard, things were much different. His body was goo, held together by a dark crust: nothing more than a charred marshmallow. Remarkably, his face had made it through the fire. The rest of his body must've bubbled in the heat, swelled and blistered and popped before crusting over.

The dead interested me: the way they lay on the sides of roads and accumulated filth on their half-naked bodies, the different positions they'd wind up in. I never could look away. I always had to stare, get my thirty-second snapshot of the scene so I could try to piece together what killed them and imagine what it must've been like to die that way. There were a lot of bodies strewn about the country, discarded, left for packs of dogs to gnaw on. The dead were everywhere, lying in the middle of paved streets, dirt roads, ransacked homes, untouched homes, ammo dumps, tree lines, desert scrub. Anywhere a person could get to, there they were, as lifeless as cinder blocks.

The city we were moving through looked like a petting

zoo. Livestock of all sorts roamed the streets: goats, sheep, and donkeys. The sheep weren't very sheepish and would nudge their noses into the backs of Marines when they crouched down beside buildings. People came out of their houses, the ones that were left standing, to watch us perform our surgery on the town. Bello steered around a pile of rubble that had once been a rather large home. The remains blocked most of the dirt street, and several Iraqis were on their hands and knees, sifting through the debris field. A group of men pointed to the rubble and yelled at us in Arabic. A young boy ran his hand across his throat at us.

"Must be Iraqi for hello," Bello said.

"Let's shoot him," I replied.

Moving through the city, I thought about driving on the beach, in a topless Jeep Wrangler, having the wind blow across my bald head, the water splashing up the sides. I'd been thinking about buying a Wrangler since Kuwait, told myself I was going to buy one when I got back, planned on using a chunk of my tax-free combat pay to get a top-of-the-line vehicle. I'd get one, then drive it to the beach so I could run into the cool Atlantic Ocean and wash away all the dirt. A random thought, yes, but one that offered a slight escape from reality.

I took a sip of water from my CamelBak and looked beyond the buildings, to the end of the street. I could see the waves breaking against the buildings. I wanted to climb down from the cramped turret and walk out to the waves. Gunshots rang out and, before I could take my daydream any farther, the waves pulled back, left only a dry beach.

The shots seemed far away, but it was hard to tell over the roar of the AAV's engine. Recon had set up shop on the other side of the city and was doing whatever it is that Recon does, which always seemed to include a bunch of ammo and a whole lot of shooting. They were always getting into something, leaving very little for the rest of us to shoot.

"Stinky, this is 302," Corporal Hall called over the radio.

"Send it," I replied.

"We need a corpsman. Two casualties. Civilians. How copy?"

"Solid copy. En route."

Bello had the vehicle turned around and moving in their direction before I could say anything to him. Hall's track had a corpsman riding on it, but he wasn't the kind of guy you'd want putting a Band-Aid on a paper cut. The grunts' corpsman rode on my vehicle and, from what we could tell, knew what he was doing.

We pulled alongside a faded blue Ford Mustang (circa 1976) that was idling in the middle of a narrow dirt road next to a canal. Hall stood next to his corpsman, who was attempting to wrap a white bandage around an Iraqi man's arm, but was having trouble keeping blood from gushing through it. His patient didn't seem bothered by the blood, and puffed on a cigarette while Doc continually wrapped and unwrapped the wound. I climbed down from my vehicle. Hall pointed to the passenger's seat before I made it to him. In it was another man. Bloodstained hands covered his blood-drenched face.

The passenger rocked back and forth in his seat in a gentle rhythmic motion.

"Damn, he's calm," I said to Hall. "Did Doc hit him up with morphine?"

"No, he didn't do anything. See the other one?"

"Must be in shock," I said.

"Not sure, but he's got a pretty good one, right through the eye. What he needs is a good corpsman. Not some jack-ass."

The grunt corpsman set his medical kit down on the ground and then squatted beside the man. He said something in a low voice to the Iraqi, pulled the man's hands away from his face. A river of blood bubbled from where his eye had been, rolled down his chin. Flies feasted on the man's misfortune. The grunt doc tried to wave them away, but there was no use, the flies were hungry and unwilling to back off from their human buffet.

"What happened?" I asked Hall.

"Recon," he said while pointing toward a fighting hole that was fifty meters away from where his AAV was parked. "They shot him."

There were only two bullet holes in the windshield, and the Marine who had so skillfully placed the 5.56 was standing waist high in a fighting hole, clutching the rifle he had used to stop the car. He watched Doc work on one of the men he'd shot. I could tell the Marine was young, probably only a lance corporal. Because he was a recon Marine, it most likely wasn't his first time shooting an Iraqi, but chances are it was the first time he'd had to stare at the damage he'd created, watch the blood slime out of the humans he'd shot.

"Nice shooting."

The grunt doc wrapped the Iraqi's head in gauze, then raised a canteen to the man's lips. A fine example of irony: Get shot in the face by the Americans and get treated by the Americans. The man tensed up, focused on the area where my ocean had been.

"Is he going to live?" I asked the corpsmen.

"Shit, I don't know. Maybe. Ain't nothing more I can do for him. We'll have to medevac him or he's going to die for sure."

It was out of my hands. Helicopter fuel isn't cheap. A higher authority would have to authorize the medevac of an Iraqi civilian. I called Gunny, who in turn called a CO. "Leave him," they ordered. "We've got a time hack to make. It's Recon's problem, not ours."

"Doc," I yelled, "better tell him to start praying."

Whether he lived or died made no difference to me. I didn't shoot him, and even if I had, I probably wouldn't have bothered to stop and look at the damage. I would've kept going, buried the thought away, and pretended it never happened. That was the easy way, and really the only way, to get through combat operations. You had to make it impersonal and tell yourself you didn't give a shit one way or another, even though you really did. It would eventually catch up to you. Sooner or later you'd have to contend with those sights and sounds, the blood and flies. But that wasn't the place for remorse. There was too much war left. We still had a lot of killing left to do.

I looked at the half-dead Iraqi, then at the young Marine who'd shot him. "Damn, at least the Iraqi got some morphine."

My dog walked back into the room. She stared up at me. Kipper handed a photo album to Paxson, then stood up and headed out the door.

"Hold on. What are you doing?" I asked.

"Getting out of here. You're skipping the good parts. What about Nasiriyah?"

"What about it?"

"That's the place you think about the most, right?"

"Yeah, I guess," I said.

Paxson pulled a picture out of the photo album and held it up. "This should help refresh your memory," he said. I knew what he was trying to show me and didn't have to look, but did. "Just keep going," he said.

Gunny yelled for me. I jogged in the direction of his voice. The sun had all but disappeared and only slivers of its rays could be seen shooting up from the skyline. Marines, vehicles, and gear were everywhere, making it hard to find anybody. Dressed in a green chemical-protective suit, flak jacket, and

Kevlar helmet, I zigzagged through the obstacles, toward his voice, that unmistakable voice.

"C'mon," Gunny said. "We've got a brief to go to." He grabbed hold of my flak jacket collar, shook it back and forth. "Time to get our kill on."

Task Force Tarawa had already leapfrogged us and moved in to the city. Nothing was supposed to happen. But something had happened, and we could hear the sounds of that something happening all around us, could smell the fighting. We were next in line. Something was about to happen to us as well.

"Got an ink stick?" Gunny asked.

"Yes, Gunny," I said.

"Bring one for me?"

"No, Gunny."

"Buddy fucker. Good thing I brought my own."

Captain Reid, the company commander of Lima Company and the man who inherited our misfit platoon of trackers, stepped in front of the school circle. You couldn't say much bad about the guy, or any of his Marines. He ran a tight ship and didn't put up with nonsense. If the captain didn't put a boot in your ass, First Sergeant Ruff would. The men assembled wouldn't need that kind of treatment; we were the company's leadership, and knew better. The group went silent, prepared to copy down notes for the mission.

"Task Force Tarawa has been ambushed," the captain said. We were already well aware of the ambush, had heard about it on the BBC. Listening to reports of a war we could hear in real life had a *Twilight Zone* quality to it, especially since we knew we were heading right into the middle of it all. We also knew that a convoy from the Army had made a wrong turn and were feared captured. We would find out later it was the 507th Maintenance Company, Jessica Lynch's crew. They'd made a wrong turn in Nasiriyah, which set the tone for one of the bloodiest battles of the Iraq war for the rest of us who were able to read a map.

Thundering booms from a nearby artillery battery and the miscellaneous sounds of combat drifted toward our virgin ears. The captain yelled so we could hear him.

"Gents, they are slugging it out in there. They've taken lots of casualties already. We're running the gauntlet, so be prepared to take more as we go in. Have your men ready to move out in a few hours but be prepared to move out in minutes."

Most of my men were teenagers and not really men at all: boys who had wanted to do something different with their lives; boys who wanted a little more adventure than most people could handle. None of us were the best and the brightest—at least not in the traditional sense. Typically, those kinds of people don't join the Marine Corps. No, we were the kind of guys who took wood shop when we were in high school rather than advanced placement courses. Street fighters, thugs, drunks, and rednecks, that's what we were. Those are the kinds of people who enlist in the Marines.

Smart people join the Air Force and, for the same pay, live the good life.

Third Section was already huddled in an AAV, passing rumors between them. "Lock it," Corporal Hall ordered the section when I walked onto the vehicle. They stopped talking, turned their attention to me. Their faces were black from days of accumulated dirt, with uniforms that looked as if they had been used to mop the desert. Nobody had gotten much sleep since the war began, and food was scarce, since the supply lines had been left behind days before. We were all tired, hungry, and dirty, but still the junior Marines didn't complain much. None of them looked like boys anymore. None of them ever would again.

I dropped my Kevlar on the center bench seat and opened my notebook to the page that contained the operation brief notes. There was no use in minimizing anything; they needed to know the possibilities, how bad things were expected to get. Worst-case scenario and hope it wouldn't come down to that. I gave them the rundown, informed them of the casualty count that had already accumulated, how many more we anticipated, and what they needed to do if somebody got hit. Really, we had a simple mission: We'd drive down a stretch hardball in single file, flank when given the command, and then shoot everything that fit in with our rules of engagement. How much could I say about that?

Hoping to motivate third section, I pulled out the all-hands message Major General James N. Mattis had given to the First Marine Division before we departed Kuwait. If the words from a Marine with the nickname "Mad Dog" couldn't evoke a little inspiration, then I was pretty sure a Marine with the call sign of Stinky wouldn't be able to do much good. I unfolded the message, cleared my throat for effect, and began to read from the paper:

> When I give you the word, together we will cross the Line of Departure. Close with those forces that choose to fight, and destroy them. Be the hunter, not the hunted. Never allow your unit to be caught with its guard down. Use good judgment and act in the best interests of our nation.
>
> You are part of the world's most feared and trusted force. Engage your brain before you engage your weapon. Share your courage with each other as we enter the uncertain terrain north of the Line of Departure. Keep faith in your comrades on your left and right and Marine Air overhead. Fight with a happy heart and strong spirit.
>
> For the mission's sake, our country's sake, and the sake of the men who carried the Division's colors in past battles—who fought for life and never lost their nerve—carry out your mission and keep your honor clean. Demonstrate to the world there is "no better friend, no worse enemy" than a U.S. Marine.

"All right, that's all I have." Artillery amped up their rate of fire, bombarded the city with even more of the 155mm rounds. The Marines were captivated by the booms and having a hard time concentrating on anything else. "Does anyone have any questions?" Nothing. The noise generated by the battle said it all.

Third section dispersed. I climbed into the turret. The two machine guns were cleaned to perfection. They had to be. Staring at the weapons, I contemplated what I was going to have to do with them. "Please don't fail me," I whispered to the weapons. Time, and a bridge that spanned the Euphrates, were the only things separating us from Nasiriyah. I stuffed a pinch of chewing tobacco into my mouth, donned my communications helmet, and began to prepare for the mission. Sliding deeper into the weapons station, I closed my eyes and tried to pray.

Our Father, who art in heaven . . .

The Lord's Prayer was the only prayer I knew. Even though I'd done some time in church when I was younger, I never paid much attention to what was being said. It really wasn't my thing. But with a battle just around the corner, I needed to think of something. So I recited the one prayer I knew, the one my high school wrestling team used to recite before our dual meets.

And forgive us our trespasses . . .

The platoon radio interrupted my prayer, which was okay since I'd been fumbling through it and couldn't remember how the rest went anyway.

"All AAVs, all AAVs. This is Buckeye. Prepare to move out. How copy?" One by one each section leader answered the call.

"First, solid," Sterlachini said.

"Second, solid," Camacci said next.

"Third, solid," I replied.

Changing my thoughts from prayer to war, I spun the turret to the right, looked back at my section of AAVs, and put my thumb in the air. Each of the crew chiefs responded by imitating me. Four vehicles. Four thumbs. Time to go. Our line of vehicles moved forward, carried us a little closer to the commotion responsible for the deaths of so many U.S. troops. Marines and soldiers from rear-echelon units had gathered along the edges of the road. Flames from a burning gas station lashed the darkness next to a huge sign that had Arabic script written across it along with a lone English word: WELCOME. I doubt we were the type of visitors the Nasiriyah chamber of commerce had in mind.

Our vehicles picked up speed. Men on the ground pumped their fists in the air as we rushed past. If I hadn't been so nervous, I might have laughed at just how cheesy it was to have those guys lined up along the sides of the road like cheerleaders, yelling our vehicles into combat. It was easy for them to get excited—they weren't heading into a hostile city.

As we crossed the bridge, the sounds of war increased. The light show began, unfolded like a Fourth of July fireworks display. Instincts formerly unknown surfaced. The vehicles continued to roll; my thoughts raced just as fast. I thought about everything we had practiced in the desert, all the training I had received as a Marine.

"Left, left, left. Turn left, dumb-ass," Gunny yelled over the platoon freq. "Goddamn it, motherfuckers. Get back on

71

the fucking road." One of the vehicles from first section had veered off the road and crashed into a light pole. Gunny was trying to get them back into the fight, but the vehicle kept running into things along the way. I could tell from his voice that he was pissed and that he was already thinking of ways to make the crew chief pay. It wasn't a good start to our first combat experience.

Each turret was equipped with a night sight, which worked pretty well when the vehicles were stationary. However, the sights were nearly impossible to use while moving, and you risked knocking your eye out in rough terrain. With our turrets buttoned up there wasn't any other choice. If I wanted to see what was going on, I had to make the best of the fuzzy green view the night sight offered and try not to lose an eye while looking through it. Still, Bello had it worse. He had the misfortune of having to *drive* while looking through night vision.

"We're taking fire."

I held on to the side of the turret with one hand and cupped my other hand around the end of the sight to use as a buffer. Bello had the vehicle going full speed and each bump he hit tossed me back and forth against the inside of the turret. Think tumble dry. Buildings became visible. Muzzle flashes erupted from the buildings. The view through the sight warped my depth perception, but I could tell the flashes were close. Too close. Each second of movement only brought them closer.

"All AAVs, flank left." The AAVs turned left, simultaneously, into the center of the city, and then stopped. The grunts dismounted, took up positions along the road. Bullets flared from the weapon stations, raced through the night, searched for victims. Automatic fire, thunderous booms from friendly tanks, my rattling turret, and the thick layer of smoke drifting over the battlefield made it hard to distinguish what was happening. A smorgasbord of emotions, dirt, and bullets gave it an unrealistic, almost cinematic, feel. We were taking rounds, yes, but I wasn't sure from where. They seemed to be coming from all directions.

"I've been shot! I've been shot!" somebody yelled through the radio. Silence. Then another call. "Warrior One down, Warrior One down."

What the hell was going on? Only five minutes into our first combat mission and already two calls of Marine casualties had been reported. Who'd be next? Something moved in the building in front of me. It could have been anything, anyone. Bello called over. He'd seen it, too. I gritted my teeth. My temples pulsed. I pushed the trigger of the fifty, watched tracer rounds crash into the building and work their way up into a window. I elevated and traversed, sent another long burst downrange. The grunts on the ground added to the melee, hit the same structure with tens of thousands of dollars' worth of firepower. Nothing could have survived the barrage, nothing. Smoke rose from the weapon, filled the turret. Ammo links spun like tops on the floor of the AAV. I shook a hot casing off my sleeve and looked through the sight. No movement. So I waited. Held my fire and waited.

It was dark one moment, and then morning the next. It was the fastest and slowest twelve hours of my life. With the sun up, I could see the damage we'd created, see the building we'd pulverized, and the many bodies that were scattered throughout the city.

I spent the dark hours with an eye pressed against the night sight, traversing and elevating my weapons. During the day, I kept my head out of the turret, eyes glued to a pair of binoculars.

While searching for more things to shoot, I noticed a scraggly dog sitting in the middle of a dirt road behind my vehicle. It wasn't the dog that caught my attention but the rounds that kept impacting around him. I moved the binos in the direction the shots were coming from, thinking I'd find a depraved Iraqi with an AK I'd be able to save the dog from. But it was a Navy corpsman pointing his pistol toward the dog and squeezing rounds off. He was a lousy shot, and too far out for the 9mm, which was a good thing for him, since Gunny Yates was heading in his direction. Shooting a person was one thing, but shooting a helpless dog was completely uncalled for. With friends like that, who needed enemies?

Two vehicles away, Kipper had his belly resting against the top of his AAV, lying in the prone position with his cheek squeezed against the side of an M16. He slid his right index finger into the trigger well, put the tip of that finger on the trigger. His body expanded when he took a deep breath. I knew what was coming next. I waited for him to exhale, and then watched a round exit the end of his rifle. Kipper connected with a shoulder. A man fell. Kipper drew in another deep breath, pulled the trigger again. He looked over at me when the smoke cleared. "Is this what you wanted?" I yelled. Corporal Kipper walked off the battlefield and back into my home office in Phoenix. He stuffed his rifle into my memorabilia box and then patted my dog on the head.

"Not really," he said.

"You said go back. I did. What the hell do you want from me?"

"I don't want anything. This isn't about what *I* want. None of this was my idea."

"Then what's the problem?"

"Well, you pussyfoot around everything. You are supposed to be a writer. Stop being a bitch and tell the fucking story. The whole story."

"I'm trying."

"There's not much we can do for you. This is your deal, you've got to figure this one out on your own, find *your* resolution."

Kipper slapped the back of my neck and then disappeared. Paxson followed. Kipper was right, I was leaving something out. I turned around and stared at the computer monitor. The remains of a Marine flashed across the screen; sounds of a firefight poured through the speakers. I rubbed my hands over the keyboard and began to type.

5

SOMEWHERE, SOMETIME, IN THE heat of that first engagement, I saw her: a small Iraqi girl, black hair, wearing a striped shirt. She couldn't have been older than ten, just a little girl. We were both in the same situation, at different ends of the spectrum. I was there to kill her. She was there to receive the salvation I had to offer in the form of a .50 caliber bullet. Nobody else saw her, just me, and I fired on the building she ran into. I blew it to shit.

If I was the only one who saw this girl, was she even present? If she wasn't then, she is now. I've added features to her face, entered her mind, and tried to persuade myself it is all made up. If nobody else saw her, she couldn't have been there.

But she was. She is: still running between the old dilapidated buildings, running to her parents, chasing a ball, looking for her dog. Whatever she was doing, I stopped it. I wonder if she was as scared as I was.

In the mall, I see a small, black-haired girl, wearing a striped shirt. She runs from store to store, looking for me. We play hide-and-seek in my memory. She wants to tell me she isn't dead. I want to tell her she wasn't there. We are separated by a line of bullets and a ragged dirt road. A man with an Abercrombie & Fitch bag walks between us before I shoot, again. Then she disappears into my memory, into my bullets, into the fire I caused.

On the ground a dead Marine looks up and smiles, and I tell myself that he wasn't there either. But he was. I have pictures of him, whoever he was—a fly-infested torso sprawled out beside a mutilated AAV. I want to call his parents and tell them I'm sorry we left him in the dirt. "We would have brought him with us, but we were too busy," I'll say. They'll understand. We had a country to liberate, an enemy to fight. Transporting his remains would've lowered morale, taken up too much space. Nobody would've recovered from that. Fuck, I think, Marines don't leave their own behind. We pride ourselves on that. It is bred into us in boot camp, reiterated along the way. Marines don't leave Marines behind. Period, end of story. Still, his unit left him in that shit-hole city, and then we left him behind.

At his funeral, I open up the coffin. He is wearing the same tattered uniform. His legs are still gone. A Purple Heart gleams from his chest. "The Marines' Hymn" plays, and the Marines in attendance stand. We put our arms to our sides, thumbs along our trouser seams, heels together smartly, and fix our eyes straight to the front—the position of attention. It is tradition. I wonder why someone doesn't pull him out of the casket and prop him up so he can observe the tradition.

During the hymn, the little black-haired girl, wearing a striped shirt, runs by. She skips up to the casket and climbs in. Nobody sees her through the tears, the dust, the bullets. The hymn plays on:

From the halls of Montezuma,
To the shores of Tripoli;
We fight our country's battles
In the air, on land, and sea:
First to fight for right and freedom
And to keep our honor clean . . .

The lid to the casket flies open when we get to the cemetery and the little girl jumps out. She runs through the freshly mowed grass, plays in a patch of familiar dirt, looks for her burnt home. Taps cries out from a bugle as the burial detail fires a twenty-one-gun salute. The little girl perches atop a tombstone. She kicks her legs back and forth and fiddles with her short black hair. I pull out a rifle and shoot her, then dump the legless Marine's body on the ground. Everything is in its place now. She is dead; he is in the dirt. So I leave, transport myself back to the war.

It's quiet in Nasiriyah now. We did our part and fulfilled everybody's destiny. I am in the turret of my AAV, behind my .50 caliber machine gun and Mark 19 grenade launcher. Bello calls over the radio to me. He wants to pull out a video camera he brought, so he can record a few memories. It turns out we won't need the video to remember, but I like the idea and tell him not to let the others see.

"Aye, aye, Sergeant," he replies. He's discreet. He films the wreck of a city, pans down to just behind the vehicle and captures some footage of the ruined body we are about to leave.

I radio Lieutenant Frank and tell him my fifty is jammed. Captain Reid called a cease-fire five minutes ago, so I need permission to test-fire the weapon. I have to make sure it works before advancing to another city to kill more people. Everyone is ready to leave, but I get the go-ahead, anyway: permission to fire granted.

"Fire both weapons," the Lieutenant says. I study the area, looking for something to shoot. Maybe the rest of the little girl's family will pop out and allow me to finish the job. My weapons are usually accurate, so I know I could waste her sister if she would only poke her head out briefly. I cock the weapons, traverse, and fire. The turret rattles, and I can taste the residue left from the exploding rounds as I release them into the city. The first burst from the MK19 sends six to eight grenades far into the city. A little high. Perhaps I scored an indirect kill. I traverse, adjust the elevation, and fire another burst, but this time with the fifty: textbook marksmanship. The rounds hit a silver tower that is elevated ten feet off the ground and only a few feet away from a two-story tan house. Liquid gushes from the holes. The weapons are fine, but I push on the MK19's trigger again anyway. The grenades crash into the same silver tower. The liquid ignites. Flames rip into the sky and trace the flammable liquid to the ground. The fire snakes its way over to the ancient home and works its way up the structure.

One by one, our vehicles pull out and begin the retrograde. The funeral pyre rages. The vehicle behind mine swings to the right to avoid running over the dead Marine, who now has a torn sandbag draped over what's left of his body. Marines in the distance fire a twenty-one-gun salute. Gunny's vehicle is the last to pass the body, and I know he will pick him up. He wanted to pick him up.

"No time for that," I would tell the family. "They wouldn't let Gunny put him in my vehicle earlier. He said we wouldn't leave him, though."

"He's one of ours," he told me. "We're taking him." I was supposed to take him, put him in the back of my vehicle. But Gunny and I followed orders, and we left him alone in that bullet-riddled city.

I search the Internet to see if anyone I know has been killed this week. It is a matter of time, I know, before I see someone else's name on the long list. I hope I can fit into my dress blues again. Scouring the list of KIAs, I wonder what his name was. Several Marines fit the description: "U.S. Marine, Nasiriyah, killed in action, remains recovered later."

There is no such list for the little girl, just a body count.

Maybe she didn't die, I try convincing myself. She comes to me and tells me it's all right. "It was supposed to happen this way," she says. The rain pounds the roof of my house. It hardly ever rains in Phoenix, yet it rains now. I look for redemption in words and wait for my stray bullet to whiz through the window.

Later on, I try to tell someone about the girl. He doesn't want to hear it, though, and just brushes it off as shit-talking; it never happened. Everyone has issues and can't afford to take on mine. I leave it at that, and, until now, say nothing. I'm embarrassed, ashamed. What kind of guy shoots a little girl?

Staff Sergeant Beck acquired a teapot somewhere on the march to Baghdad, and in between patrols, we eat stale cookies, make coffee, and pass the time at Gunny Yates's vehicle. Gunny Donahoo concocted a drink consisting of MRE cocoa powder and instant coffee; he calls it the "Big Sissy," and we sit around drinking it and smoking our recently acquired stash of Iraqi cigarettes. I borrow a wooden ammo crate to use as a "shitter box," then dig a hole, drop trou, and flip through an old magazine.

"Goddamn! You shitting again?" Beck yells from the vehicle. I wave but continue. When I get back, they are talking about the combat action ribbons we earned. The conversation moves to Nasiriyah. It seems it has affected them as well. I mention the video camera Bello had, and the Staff NCOs order me to bring it to them. When I get back, I start the tape from the beginning. Four Marines crowd around to watch. I stay to the side drinking a Big Sissy. The tattered remains of the Marine we left behind fill the small screen of the video camera. He's still dead. It seems to bother them, too.

"He's got to erase that," I hear one of them say.

Why would we erase that, I think? He died; we left. It is one of the few facts we have documented. Nobody needed to see it on video, though. How could we forget? When will we forget? For some reason, I don't want to forget.

I watch the video in my mind and relive it. Not daily—there are other images and events that need their time. Like a VHS tape, I play through them all, rewind at the end, then start from the beginning, searching for the message, the reason. There has to be one in there. The moral of the story won't reveal itself, though. It is tucked away somewhere in my mind, sitting around drinking a Big Sissy, smoking Iraqi cigarettes, and waiting for the videotape to get to the part, the part where I kill the girl and leave the Marine. Then I will pause it and see if the black-haired girl wearing a striped shirt was really there and if I did kill her. I will pull back the sandbag, look at the Marine's name tapes, say a prayer, and load him into my vehicle anyway. But there is no controlling the movie of my mind, and it tells me what I am going to see: sometimes brief glimpses into forgotten events; sometimes new, invented memories.

6

IT WAS A DIFFERENT waiting room, in the same hospital, but just as depressing. I was there with my dead, my acronym, and my anger, hoping the psychiatry guru I was about to see would be able to guide me to clarity or at least subdue some of the anger. The room was a little bigger than the first clinic but still as homey as a cardboard box. By the looks of it, some of the veterans in the waiting room knew exactly how that box felt. Almost every chair had a body stuffed into it. I stood in the doorway, next to the entrance. I didn't plan on squeezing in next to anyone, especially the way it smelled in there.

One might expect a little more camaraderie among the

crazy, but nobody in the room said anything. Only a murmur of noise came from the lady at the reception desk, who kept running her mouth to another employee while three veterans stood in front of her work space, waiting for an acknowledgment, a hi or something. No such luck. It really didn't matter; none of us would be going anywhere anytime soon.

Welcome to the Jade Clinic.

To be fair, there are a few decent clinics in the Phoenix VA. The Emerald Clinic, only one hundred yards down the hall, seemed like a different world. The nurses were friendly and my primary-care physician (PCP) always provided first-rate service. Unlike the majority of staff members in the mental-health clinic, my PCP acted like he wanted to be there and treated veterans with respect. The kind of service you'd expect the government to provide its veterans. The kind of treatment I thought we deserved.

Even the Jade Clinic's waiting room seemed inhospitable and cold. The staff's apathy fit right in with the surroundings and they seemed as if they had been specifically handpicked to dole out subpar service. *Disheartening* isn't a strong enough word to describe what I felt as I watched my fellow veterans being ignored.

To avoid embarrassment, or to keep the sane away, the clinic was tucked behind a wall and next to a line of soda machines. Only when one of the "normal" patients got thirsty enough to walk over to the machines did the lost world reveal itself, which suited me just fine since I never wanted to be spotted in that place anyway. I didn't mind keeping crazy to myself. For all I cared, they could've placed the clinic in the basement.

Not so coincidentally, the police shack was just a pill's throw away from the crazy-man clinic. Whoever designed the hospital had the right idea—put cops near the crazies. And with the kind of service the Jade Clinic offered its patients, having the two places within shouting distance seemed like a pretty good idea. The Mad Hatter's tea party came to mind.

I rested my head against the wall, listened to pages flip and people breath. Noise didn't usually bother me, but silence was something else. It was almost unbearable. I needed noise. Bad things took place during silent periods. At least during a fire-fight you have a pretty good idea of the possibilities.

The clouds covered the moon or the moon wasn't out. Since I wasn't a meteorologist or an astronomer, I knew only that it was too dark to walk far away from my AAV. If you gave the wrong password when challenged, or if the Marine who'd challenged you forgot the correct password, you easily could have gotten a bullet. Friendly fire scared me as much as enemy fire. Besides, all kinds of evil lurked in the shadows of that Baghdad construction site. The size of the rats alone would make you think twice about heading into the dark.

Unsafe in daylight, the roads were downright deadly after sundown. In order to maintain some kind of order along the roadways, every unit in the area manned its own traffic control points (TCP). Marines at the checkpoints had two jobs:

Search every vehicle they stopped and shoot any vehicle that didn't stop in time. Most of us preferred the latter to the former, since pulling the trigger seemed much safer than searching a vehicle. They way I saw it, any Iraqi daring enough to drive around town at night had a death wish of some sort and deserved whatever he received.

Besides a slight rumble coming from Corporal Hall's idling AAV, not much else could be heard. Hall and his crew watched the TCP along with a squad of grunts and two Humvees. Cut off from the unit by a small patch of trees and shrubs, they had enough firepower to sustain heavy fighting for quite some time, if needed—a good thing, since the rest of the unit had either gone to sleep or scrunched into one of the buttoned-up AAVs to play spades. Lulled by the silence, nobody thought much about anything except relaxing.

Gunny Yates, however, had his AAV's ramp lowered as usual. Something was going on at his vehicle. Staff NCOs and officers circulated through his track. I was curious about what kind of stunt Gunny had pulled and decided to brave the dark and take my chances with the rats. I ventured away from my AAV, headed for the action.

"What's going on?" I said to Gunny.

"Look inside the ammo crate," he said. "But don't let my dinner escape."

I lifted the top off the box. A scraggly chicken tilted its head up at me.

"You aren't really going to eat that, are you? It doesn't have all its feathers. You'll probably get food poisoning or AIDS or something from it."

"Less to pluck means there's less work to do," he said. "Shit, if I get sick, I get sick. We're all gonna die sometime anyway. Dying with a drumstick in my mouth doesn't sound like a bad way to go to me."

"I don't think it's a good idea."

"Oh, really, junior. I appreciate your concern and all, but how about you let me be the Gunny, and you can be the sergeant. How's that sound, Lump-Lump?"

"Can I be the Gunny tomorrow?"

He motioned for me to walk closer to him, raised his other hand in the air. I got within range. He slapped the back of my head.

"There's your answer."

The chicken cawed, then started to peck at the box. "Shut the fuck up," Gunny yelled. I leaned against the side of the vehicle, listened to Gunny talk about how he planned on seasoning and boiling the bird. A .50 cal erupted. Gunny stopped talking, looked toward the TCP. Another fifty sputtered. Small arms opened up. Gunny jumped to his feet.

"Get over there," he ordered.

"Aye, aye," I replied.

Gunny readied his vehicle. I ran through the tree line, toward Hall's vehicle. A roar echoed from the construction site as the rest of the AAVs cranked their engines.

Two grunts pointed their weapons in the window of a

beat-up truck. The driver had gotten lucky. Like a magnet, his little rusted truck had sucked the bullets away from him. The grunts pulled the unhurt Iraqi out of his truck. The man yelled in broken English, waved his hands in the air. "Shut your mouth," one of the Marines yelled back. The driver kept babbling, switching between Arabic and English. "Shut your damn mouth," the Marine ordered. They flung him to the ground, pointed their weapons in his face. Another grunt slid a sandbag over the Iraqi man's head. Then it was quiet again.

"Mr. Van Winkle," somebody said. I turned away from the hooded man, stared down the hall of the crazy-man clinic. "Come with me." I followed the doctor to his office. He closed the door behind us, wiggled into his chair.

Clack, clack, clack was about the only sound that came out of the doctor's office. He typed away on his computer, his back facing me. I sat in a chair, watched a few minutes tick off the clock. He wrote a prescription for another type of antidepressant that was supposedly good for treating PTSD. I took the paper from him, pushed it into my pocket. He asked the same questions the nurse had asked during my first visit to the clinic, suggested I take the medication like I had been told, and then sent me off. "See you in a few months," he said to me on my way out. I wouldn't have known anything about PTSD if it weren't for the Internet. An explanation would've been nice. Hell, even a brochure. Something.

7

MEN CROWDED THE STREETS to watch us work
our way through their neighborhood. Out-of-work Baathists,
Saddam fedayeen, and civilians all looked the same: dark skin,
dark hair, and civilian attire. There wasn't any way to tell if one
of them was planning on popping a round off at us as we drove
by or if they wanted to hug us when we got on the ground.
They didn't seem angry, but after the stuff we'd done to their
country, I knew they couldn't be too happy. They probably
hadn't been happy before we arrived. It was, after all, Saddam
City, the poorest area of Baghdad. If the size of the rats and
trash piles were an accurate indication, the area had long been
in disarray.

By the time my stepbrother Matt's Army unit took charge of the same area, the name of the city had changed to Sadr City, but according to Matt, the name change hadn't changed anything at all. It was still dangerous and nasty. There were other differences. We didn't have to think too much about roadside bombs, hadn't even heard of the term IED. Instead, we had to worry about being blown apart by rocket-propelled grenades and old-school tanks. So, when Matt came home from Iraq, he had a whole different set of problems to contend with: Swerving his vehicle away from trash alongside the road was a big one.

We hadn't showed up to search houses or secure anything. It was just a show of force, a tour of our new area of operation (AO). A pair of grunts walked in front of the AAV, far enough ahead so that the raw sewage coating the side of our vehicle wouldn't splash them. Mountains of rotting garbage lined the street. Bello steered around the piles. I traversed the turret into the crowd. At least two hundred Iraqi men and boys had crowded into a small square, and to be safe, I kept my weapons trained on them. How they could stand the smell, the garbage, or the sewage was beyond comprehension, but they didn't appear concerned with the health implications as they stood in the middle of the filth chain-smoking their Iraqi cigarettes. The crowd started to push forward, as if they were at a concert and we were the main act. The grunts shoved a few people, but it barely put a dent in the problem. The residents of Saddam City were accustomed to being pushed around.

New tactic: The grunts pointed their weapons and yelled

the one Arabic word we thought we knew, which was supposedly pronounced "cough" and meant "Halt." This word was preceded by a colorful word from our own language and the click of an M16's safety mechanism. The Iraqis got the point: They could step away from the Marines and live or move closer and die. We didn't want to kill anybody who didn't deserve it—at least anybody we didn't think deserved it. None of us, that I could tell, had any quarrel with the Iraqi people. We weren't pointing our weapons at them to taunt them or because we could. It wasn't like that at all. Our goal was to make it out alive.

The thick crowd clogged the tiny street, strangled our exit route. Bello stopped the AAV. The bulky vehicles were moving blind spots. He couldn't see the right side from his position in the driver's station, which was several feet away from the turret. I couldn't see the left side while I was in the turret, even though it was the highest point of the vehicle. To make things a little more interesting, neither of us could see a great deal of what was happening behind the vehicle. In those kinds of situations we had to rely on the grunts to get us through crowds. Crunching over a body wouldn't slow an AAV down the slightest, probably wouldn't be noticed by those inside. So, four grunts always stayed around the vehicle, mainly for our safety, but also for the safety of the civilians.

A grunt walking in front of the vehicle waved his hand at me and said something I couldn't hear.

"Bello," I called over the intercom system, "what's he saying?"

"Can't tell, Sergeant. But now he's pointing, too."

If one of the Iraqis did have a weapon, the grunts had a better chance of neutralizing the situation than I did. The weapons in the turret had started out accurate, but after weeks of bouncing around the desert, crashing into walls, and firing, they were better used in places that offered a little more wiggle room. While it would have been easy enough to take a person out with either of the crew-served weapons, it would've been more of a spray-and-pray operation than a surgical procedure.

Sometimes the options we had weren't good enough and we had to improve our chance of survival by improvising. We did that by keeping confiscated weapons handy—weapons collected and earmarked for use in the new Iraqi Army once it formed. Gunny Yates was loaded to the teeth and had more weapons than an entire infantry platoon. When weapons were found, they were placed in Gunny's track. And even though he was supposed to relinquish those weapons at the end of the day, he always made sure there were a few AKs stashed around his vehicle. His reasoning: If he ran out of ammo, or we found ourselves in a particularly sticky situation, he would be able to take ammo from the enemy and continue to fight. The infantry officers, however, didn't see things the same way. But since Gunny was usually right on the money, I followed his lead and kept a retractable stock AK-47 in the turret. Gunny had given me the Russian-made assault rifle a few weeks earlier with the caveat "You didn't get that from me."

With such a large crowd forming, and the mysterious

signals I was receiving from the grunt, I reached back, uncovered the weapon, and ensured that its magazine full of 7.62mm was inserted. The grunt moved closer to the vehicle, just under the turret, and mouthed something again. As usual, I couldn't hear anything, just watched his lips move.

"What?" I yelled down from the turret.

"Look," he said loud enough for me to hear over the roar of the idling engine.

"At what?"

"It's Mohammed O'Malley," he replied, smiling, obviously amused with his find.

"Who the fuck is that?"

The grunt pointed into the crowd again. I followed his hand with my eyes. A red-haired little boy was leaning against a light pole in the middle of the square. His skin glowed white. "Holy shit, you're right," I yelled back down to the grunt. The little boy was a lighthouse on a dark night, the most visible person in the entire crowd. I don't know how I missed seeing him in the first place.

"Bello," I said, "you see that shit?"

"Yeah, must suck to be him," he replied.

It couldn't have been easy being a pale-skinned, red-haired boy in Iraq. How do you blend in when you look like that, in a country like that? You don't.

A few months prior, Kipper had predicted that Iraq would change us. He said that, one way or another, we weren't going to be the same people after the war. He figured it would be for the worse, couldn't imagine life going back to normal again. I, too, understood that once I got home my life would be different. It had to be. How different, I had no way of knowing. None of us did. College, however, illuminated that change, made me feel like a redheaded Iraqi kid standing in a crowd of black-haired men. I'd become the Mohammed O'Malley of my world.

8

I HAD CLASS IN an hour, and I was either going to show up slightly buzzed or not show up at all. Either option was a possibility. I'd built up a pretty good tolerance to alcohol and thought I could weave my Jeep through anything. I was indestructible.

I'd been thinking about the Marines I'd served with. The unit was already in Iraq, slugging it out in Haditha and, unlike before, I didn't have a good feeling about them being over there. Things were so much different. It wasn't the same war I'd fought in, and very few of the Marines I served with were still in the unit. I had completed my enlistment and received an honorable discharge, but still didn't feel like I'd done enough.

Class, I thought. Yes, I'll go to class. Why not? It would give me something to do, a reason to get out of the house and escape my self-imposed imprisonment. I slid my feet into a pair of Doc Martens steel-toed boots, pulled the laces tight around my ankles, and then tied them. The habit of wearing boots was one I couldn't break. Keeping my hair short was another one.

I knew I reeked of beer and cigarettes, but didn't attempt to cover the smell with cologne. Really, there wasn't any sense in trying to mask my sins.

A handful of students huddled around computer stations, clacking away on keyboards. I stood in the middle of the room, talking to the professor. Somewhere in our conversation, Iraq was mentioned, which piqued a student's interest. I could tell she was about to say something, but hoped she wouldn't and that if I ignored her she'd go away. I didn't mind talking about the war in general terms, but didn't want to get specific, or share my memories. Not with her. Not with any of them.

"Did you kill anybody?" the student blurted out.

The keyboard clatter stopped. The rest of the students waited for a response but acted as if they hadn't heard the question. She stared at me. I looked down, ran a hand across my stubbly, bald head.

"I took part in a war," I replied.

I needed a better answer. Something not as lame. Something that let her know that I thought she was a real bitch for asking the question. I couldn't come up with anything else. Nothing that said, "Yeah, but nobody killed any of my guys. I'm home. Doesn't any of that matter?" Apparently my answer didn't satisfy her because she tried to go on, "I know, but . . ."

The professor turned his head toward her to let her know it was an inappropriate question. The girl walked away, never got the point. Never knew that she'd been rude or grasped the magnitude of the question.

The question came up often. People rarely asked if I was happy to be back or if everything was all right. They just wanted to know if I killed anybody. They see it all the time in the movies: A Marine goes to war. He runs through the jungles killing everything he comes across. Returns home victorious, gets the girl, and rides off into the sunset. There aren't any wall-pounding fits of rage or consequences in that make-believe world, just parades and happy endings.

People wanted a yes or no answer, like shooting another human was that easy. No matter what the reason, the ways I tried to justify the situation, the second-guessing that lingered, nothing could change the fact that people stopped existing because of me. How do you sum that up in a passing conversation?

Still, I tried to find ways to answer. I wanted to tell them, but couldn't. I wanted people to know that we fired rounds into moving trucks and open windows to survive, not for anyone else's freedom. Not for the Democrats. Not for Republicans. Just to survive. Because we had bullets and shooting was what we did best—pull the trigger, think about it later. The thrill of it all wore off along the way. Getting everyone home alive trumped all.

"Did you kill anyone?"

"Goddamn right. I wasted a group of men. A corpsman tried to shoot a dog. The unit in front of us accidentally mowed down a bus packed with civilian women and children, left them to rot in the desert. Little hands draped out of red-stained windows, bodies limp on their dead mothers' laps—a full bus, all dead. Yeah, we fucking killed. One of our Marines shot a burst of .50 cal into a crowd of armed looters. Another Marine used his .50 cal to eliminate a shadowy figure he saw lurking in a building. It was a perfectly fired burst, through a window and into a living person. Man, you should've seen that. It was something out of a horror movie: red mist and chunks of flesh. We talked about the scene for weeks."

It wouldn't have mattered how I replied, she still wouldn't have gotten it. More questions would have followed, until I found myself back over there. Back in the dirt, dodging RPGs and gunfire. Shooting whatever moved, surviving.

A man kept poking his head out from around the corner of a building. He was just to my left, a couple of hundred yards in front of the vehicle. I traversed the turret and sighted in on him. I could've pulverized his body with either of the weapons. He disappeared behind the building again. I couldn't tell what he was doing, but he kept moving back and forth, playing hide-and-seek with me. Was he laughing? Holding a GPS? Calling in our grid coordinates? I applied pressure to the butterfly trigger, not too much, but just enough. He was about to get a burst of .50 cal rounds sent his way. While I could've shot through the corner of the building, I didn't. Instead I continued to watch him.

"Clint, don't hesitate," is the advice my dad gave me before I left for Iraq. "Come home. Figure it out later," he said.

I kept thinking about thinking. I was doing too much of it. I could've shot and gotten away with it even though the only true threat was in my head. *Don't hesitate.*

When I applied more pressure to the butterfly trigger, the man's light-colored *dishdasha* bloomed into a red masterpiece. I kept shooting, brushing red onto the human canvas. I wiped my eyes and looked through the scope again. He was on the ground, but my hand was still pushing the trigger, sending a prolonged burst of rounds into his body. I shot until he turned to paste. All his insides were out, his hair scattered in the wind. Body parts flew into the air. A piece of ear landed in the gulley, a fingertip bounced off the side of a house. The corner of the building had ripped away and mixed with what was left of his body. I kept shooting but he wouldn't die. He just stared through my sights, laughing at me. I could barely see anything through all the fog I'd created but still wouldn't release the trigger. The erupting, smoking, vibrating of the weapons was exhilarating, euphoric.

Bello yelled through the intercom system for me to stop shooting. Even though he was two ranks lower than me, he was yelling, "Sergeant, stop. Stop fucking shooting. He's dead. Stop fucking shooting." The man was merely a stain on the earth, but I couldn't stop shooting.

That only happened in my head. In reality, I never shot. I hesitated; just stared at the dark-skinned man in the light-colored *dishdasha* and kept telling myself to fire rounds into him. He's going to kill us all, I kept thinking. He could've. And even though I never shot the man, I still see him, even dream about him. However, now he chases *me* through the alleys of *my* country: around Phoenix, through Orlando, and down the Virginia Beach shoreline. He has a rifle sighted in on me and all I can do is run. I still think about shooting him and what it would've been like to turn him into paste. Would he still chase me now if I'd shot him then?

I wanted to kill him. I still want to kill him.

I think maybe I should have killed more people when I had the chance. I think maybe I should have killed fewer. I missed so many opportunities to fire. I took too many. Bodies certainly fell because of my actions, but I never had to see the people I ripped apart. I mainly viewed the death others created. I was lucky: My war was an impersonal war full of indiscriminate firing and long-distance death, for the most part. I was protected by the distance my long-range weapons afforded, given the chance to kill without having to see much of the aftermath of *my* killing sprees.

When I thought about the war, I was glad I was home. Then I'd go outside and smoke a cigarette and think about how much I missed it all. It didn't make any sense. I still wanted to go back, and could have, but was afraid that I wouldn't make it out alive a second time. Afraid I'd lost my edge and would get others killed. My mind wandered too much and I wasn't sure I would be able to get back into all of it or if I had enough restraint left to be able to make rational decisions. But I wanted to go back. Sometimes, I still do.

I missed the war and the freedom that came with it. When you are that close to death, you feel free. Every breath you take could be your last. So you inhale and savor each breath, try not to think about your death even though signs of it are all around you. The freedom comes from knowing that if anybody gives you crap, you can eliminate them and the situation. Just shoot and get it over with. You are the entire legal system behind the sights of your weapon and you just focus and wait for your turn to make the red mist and pray it doesn't happen to you first.

After I rotated back to that strange place called the civilian world, I was among those who'd never had the chance to taste that type of freedom, the feelings soured and curdled inside of me. The dead morphed from hajis into "real people" and I was alone with my memories of how those people were splattered and smashed and blown apart. The last thing I wanted was to have them resurrected in the middle of a university classroom by a girl who was worrying about math exams while I was off fighting in a war.

This is true: The grunts had been shooting at a group of men hiding behind a wall. Every once in a while the grunts would see the top of a head pop up from behind the structure and would unload hundreds of rounds of ammunition into the wall. It was a small, unimpressive barrier, set between two homes, and parallel to the road but three hundred meters away from my position. The wall was most likely older than me, maybe older than my country, and weathered from years of sandstorms. The grunts thought they'd hit a few of the men, but weren't sure because their rifles weren't punching through the hefty stone structure. So they yelled up at me and pointed toward the wall. I never saw the Iraqis but gave a thumbs-up and slid down into the turret.

I worked the fifty along the wall, moving it up and down, throwing chunks of stone into the air with each burst fired. Then I switched over to the forty mike-mike. The wall didn't stand a chance against the high explosive dual-purpose grenades, and with a five-meter casualty radius, neither did anybody behind the wall. A single burst knocked a section of the thing down.

Lance Corporal Meyers handed two boxes of ammo up from the back of the vehicle, then started to gather spent casings off the floor. I traversed the turret and fired ten rounds into the portion of the wall that was still standing. Rounds glided through each time I pushed on the butterfly trigger. I popped out of the turret to get a better view, then shot more without using the sights, worked my way around the wall like a graffiti artist, leaving my mark along the ancient structure. It only took five minutes to eliminate ten or so lives with two boxes of ammunition—pretty good math.

I never saw them. I can imagine they weren't there.

Those were stories I could've told the girl when she asked if I'd killed anybody. Maybe I was being too hard on her and she was genuinely interested in the war but didn't know how to ask. Perhaps, by answering her, I could've let her know that the shooting and killing weren't as black-and-white as most people think. The actions live in that hazy area of blown-apart stone walls and hesitations. Sometimes I shot when I shouldn't have; other times I didn't shoot when I should have. There was no way to explain why I did either. Everything happened so fast. Decisions had to be made. After I got home I began to see things in slow motion, see the actions that might've been mistakes. But there was no way for that girl to understand, and I knocked her down like the Iraqi wall when I could've given her a brief lesson on the fog of war. There was a time when I wanted to know the same things, when I thought combat was as simple as pulling the trigger.

My grandpa never talked about World War II to anyone. The family knew he had served in the Army but not much else. After I became a Marine, he started to tell stories about his war to me. It was a "good war"—the other "war to end all wars" that didn't end any wars. I found out he served overseas for three years, dug fighting holes in occupied Berlin, got in bar fights in France, and spent time in Wales. He talked about going and coming, his Army buddies and training, but never got into the stuff I really wanted to know. Had he ever killed anybody? Had he been granted the "privilege" of taking the life of another in combat? To me, killing was the important part, the part that mattered. That was war, right? Finally I asked him.

His reply confused me. It was cryptic and unsatisfying. I'd expected to hear about him bayoneting a Nazi or kicking somebody's teeth in. More than that, I expected to hear a gleeful recollection of it all. Instead, I got an account of how he shot at a German sniper.

His engineer unit was doing what engineers do when rifle rounds started to impact around their bivouac area. Not many rounds, just a few. My grandpa found concealment and returned fire with his M1 Garand rifle. Up to that point in the story, I was with him and extremely happy to hear that a Van Winkle had "gotten one." But that wasn't the part I found confusing; it was how he ended the story. After shooting at the German, who eventually fell out of a tree, he walked over to where the sniper lay. The German, sprawled out and riddled with bullet holes, was dead. Here's the kicker, though: Instead of being happy, Grandpa was relieved to see that the German soldier had more holes in him than he had fired. That was the end of the story. Maybe he killed the guy, maybe he didn't. Grandpa didn't want to know either way, and, at the time, I couldn't understand why.

When I got back from Iraq, and saw my grandpa, we talked about war again. However, we talked about it in a different manner than we had years earlier. We talked about the places we saw and the friends we gained. We bypassed the death and shooting. Our wars were sixty years apart but weren't really any different. It didn't matter how many years separated our wars or where we traveled to fight them. Blood still dried the same way around wounds and charred bodies still crusted over the same as they always have. It didn't matter that he'd fought in a "good war" and I fought in a controversial war, because the effect turned out to be the same: Neither of us could find anything praiseworthy about combat.

I understood the silent portions of our conversation, what was said when nothing was said at all. The true stories hid in the silence. Instead of being grandson and grandpa, we were just two combat vets who understood what war does and the importance of being around others who don't have to ask questions.

In war, no one asks you if you killed anyone. You don't have to say anything after a firefight. You just come back and sit around with your fellow Marines. All you have to do is nod and they know. The questions are answered because you are there together. They know and you know. Nobody asked why one of us shot into that window or why the unit in front of us ripped into that bus or why I shot the group of men hiding behind that wall. Everything was understood.

Maybe it wasn't the war itself but the people who were in the war with me I missed. Perhaps all I really wanted was to know it was all right and worth it and that my actions were justified. I wanted to be back in the company of others who understood what it's like to pull the trigger. Wanted to get away from the questions and the made-up answers—to get back to a place where I felt normal again.

There was nothing normal about college. I'd seen too much to be able to relate with other students. I didn't want to answer their questions, but, in a way, I needed to answer them. I felt a responsibility to the guys who hadn't made it home. If that wasn't enough, I was also lugging around those four letters the nurse had bestowed upon me at the VA. PTSD: It was just one more thing to think about, to try to make sense of.

The students remained quiet for the rest of the session. I felt like the story in that journalism class. They typed. I thought. The questioning girl resumed her normal life. The professor, Peter Aleshire, seemed to look for something to say, a way to ask if everything was okay, if the girl's question had bothered me. Pete must've known it had. He'd been a journalist for too long not to be able to read people.

My professors at Arizona State University challenged me to think about the situation I'd been in, to not take everything at face value. I could regurgitate what I had been told, and what I was being told, but nothing would be solved. To get to the bottom of it all, to really understand my experience, the answers would have to come from within. Introspection, however, wasn't always a pleasant experience, especially when I started to question everything I had once so vehemently believed in.

I stopped at the usual Mexican restaurant on the way home from school. The waitress dropped off a bowl of chips and a margarita on the rocks, extra salt. Right away, I ordered another one, knowing that it wouldn't take long to get through the first. Enclosed and away from the world, the dark booth was comforting. Alone: Just a margarita and me. The glasses accumulated, left little room for anything else. I pushed them into a wedge formation and prepared an assault on the napkin holder.

Names of the war dead for the week scrolled across the bottom of the big-screen television. I stopped moving the glasses around long enough to watch the names slide across. No matter how many times I saw the different list of dead troops, I never got used to it or the feeling that maybe I should have been included. I wasn't familiar with any of the names, but that hardly meant anything to me. I didn't have to know the dead personally to know what kind of stuff they had participated in. I mourned each as if he had been a personal friend, and the grief took a toll on me.

I ordered a shot of tequila, slammed it down straight. I rolled the shot glass in the palm of my hand, got ready to throw it at the television screen.

My head swirled, but I was still contemplating another drink. Maybe all the drinking was becoming a problem. Maybe

I had too much time on my hands. Even though I was taking twenty-one hours each semester, and on my way to earning a bachelor of arts degree, with honors, in only two and a half years, I was bored—like being stuck in Kuwait without anything to do. It was easy to understand why Gunny always had us doing something: tromping through the desert without AAVs, taking written tests, erecting cammie nets over borrowed vehicles, whatever. He must've known that boredom brings problems, allows too much time to think. So, besides preparing us for war, was he also protecting our minds? Keeping us sharp and focused by not allowing us to think too much about what was going to happen once we made it into Iraq?

In some messed-up way, being home produced withdrawal symptoms. I'd experienced the most exciting events of my life. Nothing could ever compare to the feelings war induced. Nothing. I'd never get the same adrenaline rush or create the kinds of bonds we Marines had with each other. Civilian life was dull compared to what I'd done.

"What are you doing?" asked a guy sitting across from me. His tan and brown desert cammies contrasted with the maroon booth. Dark stains covered the bottom of the shredded uniform.

"Drinking," I said.

I didn't recognize the Marine. His features were blurred, undistinguishable. I squinted hard, tried to make a connection. He could've been anybody, but something made me think that we knew each other.

"Don't recognize me without the sandbag over my head,

do you?" he said. He leaned back, draped his shattered left arm over the top of the booth. Flies swarmed around his crusted eyes. He didn't look the same, not sitting up. The last time I saw him he was sprawled out in the dirt, about to be left behind in Nasiriyah.

"You say it like it was nothing," I replied.

"Not much I can do about it."

"Guess not."

"You know, you're lucky; it could've been worse. Look how it turned out for me," he said.

"Maybe you are the lucky one," I replied.

"Fuck off! You got to come home and see *your* family. You're screwing off in college, for Christ's sake. And it's not like you're out curing cancer either. You're a goddamn English major. C'mon, how hard can that be? You need to suck it up. Stop being so damn unappreciative and lose the anger."

He was right. What did I have to complain about? I needed to stop being such a prick. But I wasn't unappreciative. If anything, the war had made me appreciate life more, helped me see what was important. It was just hard to express that appreciation when all I could think about was Iraq. There was no escaping it. Iraq was everywhere.

"Move on, Clint," I said to myself. "It's over. Leave it alone."

The Marine was gone when I looked up, had marched back into my chaotic mind. I polished off the rest of the chips and stumbled out of the restaurant.

True, it was over. But in some respects the war had become more real than it had been while I was in Iraq. There wasn't much time for reflection while we were in country. I never stopped to think about what it all meant, or really even cared. It wasn't until I got home and started talking to the dead, revisiting the war, that anything started to sink in. Was it worth it? I don't know. That's up to the dead to decide.

When I'm an old man and all the dreams and sights have left my head, when the memories are stolen from me, then historians will tell us whether it was worth it or not—if the war really helped anybody. Until then, I'll live with the dead. We'll carpool together. Do lunch and late-night snacks. Slumber parties and drinking binges. It really won't matter what anyone says, or if the whole stinking operation finally gets labeled a "good war." It was too late for me. The dead and I were together.

9

BIRDS DROPPED FROM THE trees into the dew-saturated grass to search for their morning chow. Rays from the morning sun filtered in through a set of vertical blinds that were pulled tight across a sliding glass door in my living room. The night had come and gone with little fanfare. I couldn't remember the last time I slept. However, insomnia wasn't all bad. My lack of sleep meant I had more time to get things done and was always awake to see Sara before she headed off for her teaching internship at whatever elementary school the university had her slaving in that particular semester.

I'd managed to get a lot accomplished in the dark hours.

I'd written a story (and then purposely deleted it), packed a lunch for Sara, made a meatloaf for that night's dinner, washed the dishes I'd dirtied, and then gathered up all the empty five-gallon bottles we used for our watercooler (Sara thought Phoenix's tap water tasted like dirt) and loaded the containers into my Jeep. The water station was a few blocks away, just in front of the Mexican restaurant, which, unfortunately, wouldn't be open for several hours.

I pulled my Jeep into the parking lot next to the water refilling station. Flashing lights from a Phoenix police cruiser reflected off the windows. Hypnotized by the strobe light effect and the reason the cops were present, I stepped out of my vehicle, walked to the edge of the street with the bottles in hand. A body lay in the gutter on the far side of the road. The bus shelter behind the dead man looked like a Jackson Pollock painting: the red pattern splattered across its Plexiglas encasing looked all too familiar. I stared at the mess. A plainclothes police officer stood over the body with a camera while three uniformed officers stopped and turned around oncoming traffic. Flashes from the camera turned into explosions. Red flares rocketed into the pink morning sky. The dead man sat up and waved at me. I didn't flinch, just began to move forward, toward the body, the blood, and the officers.

Lance Corporal McDaniels was already on the other side of the road, walking behind the officers. He stepped over the corpse, which was in remarkably good condition for a man who, I assumed, had been squashed by a car of some sort and died in the middle of a street. McDaniels, one of the younger Marines in my section, continued forward with his eyes fixed on the ground. He picked up a discarded Burger King bag, pulled out a handful of soggy fries, and then stuffed them into his mouth.

We hadn't been resupplied in a week and had depleted our stash of chow. One MRE a day was the most anyone could expect. If you were lucky, you'd at least get one. So, unless the Marines found something on the side of the road after completing their at-halt checks, they'd just have to go without. "Horse, saddle, man," Gunny always said to the platoon. (You were supposed to take care of your ride, then your weapons, and if you had enough time afterward, yourself.) A whole line of young Marines was walking along the side of the hardball with McDaniels, kicking through the rubbish other units had thrown on the road, hoping to locate half an MRE cracker or a misplaced pound cake hidden in the debris that had been left behind. I doubted all of them had taken care of their horses or saddles, doubted any of them cared about anything else besides making an offering to their stomach pangs. Watching some of the best-trained military men in the world scouring through garbage for food only enforced what I already knew: Hunger is a powerful force, one that will drive people to do things they would ordinarily shy away from. Gunny had urged the platoon to stop eating their allotted three meals a day while in Kuwait, in order to get accustomed to what he knew was going to happen. Apparently, not everyone listened.

"Mount up," Gunny yelled to the Marines. They tossed down the trash they had been rifling through, stuffed any chow they'd found into their cargo pockets, and ran back to their assigned vehicles. The team of Phoenix police stayed put, kept on processing the crime scene even though exhaust fumes from the platoon of AAVs had begun to blanket the scene and engulf the police officers. We pulled around the dead man's body, past the blinking squad cars, and headed down the hardball.

Tinted sun/wind/dust goggles shielded my eyes. I held on to the sides of the turret to keep from getting flung out. Bello was good driver and usually kept the ride smooth, but every once in a while he'd hit a pothole or have to veer the vehicle off the road to keep from running over one of the many bloated bodies that had been liberated from an oppressive dictator. Not many other drivers felt bad about squishing the dead with an AAV, but extracting clothing and body parts from the steel tracks was a hassle that made the activity not worth the time.

For some reason, we were circling back to secure the same stretch of road we'd secured two days prior. Going to the same place twice seemed to be standard operation procedure, and nobody was ever happy about it, especially not Gunny Yates, who had visions of being the *very* first Marine in Baghdad. But looping back was what we had been slated to do, and, like just about everything else, it was out of our control.

While not much was under our control, at the same time, so much was. It was just one of the many contradictions of war.

Cheers of "Good Bush" had roared from crowds of smiling locals the first time we drove through that village. Groups of men and boys waved from outside their homes, gave the universal sign for peace, and pumped their fists in elation. Why don't they stay inside like the rest of their countrymen and wait for the bombs to come and get them, I thought? Get off the fucking streets, stop waving, stop enticing my section into thinking the war is nothing more than one big parade through the desert.

The next time we passed through, the same area was different. The locals had lost their hospitality and had become somewhat hostile (mainly in a passive-aggressive way). Children stared up at me and ran their grimy little Iraqi fingers across their throats when my vehicle drove by. Obviously the little fuckers didn't know the capabilities of the loaded weapons I had or that any other military force would've just eliminated them from the earth for those gestures. Saddam certainly wouldn't have put up with such nonsense.

A group of Iraqis had gathered at the edge of town. They inched closer to the road when they saw our tracks and started to jeer the column, mocking the Marines as they passed. One little boy configured his hand into the shape of a gun—thumb up, index finger extended—and pointed it at Sterlachini's vehicle, which was the lead AAV. Pathetic considering none of us had to pretend we had weapons. The world slowed and everything seemed to be amplified. Dirt particles looked like boulders. The group wasn't going to shoot at us, I was pretty sure. They were only antagonizing the people who had been sent to die in their tuberculosis-infested country. If they wanted to play games, I was willing to play. I reached down into the turret, put my hand on the traverse switch, and readied myself for our approach.

Traveling through the nondescript town, I felt myself tiring of war. Exhausted from trying to figure out what was going on, why we really had to be there and who actually liked us. "Some of these people smile. Some are just showing their teeth," Corporal Hall would say. I was tired of trying to figure out which one of the two they were doing, tired of fighting for an ungrateful group of people and putting my ass on the line for their freedom.

Infuriated by the gesture being made by the junior cub insurgent, I hit the traverse switch a few feet in front of him. My turret spun. The sudden movement of the weapons swinging in their direction caused the group to scatter. I wasn't going to shoot, but how were they supposed to know what my intentions were? They disappeared into the city, leaving behind the sun-baked corpse of a middle-aged man. Another road, another body. It wasn't disfigured enough to warrant a look.

Lights from the Phoenix police cruisers were visible again. A car sped by, stopped me from stepping off the curb and into the street. The plastic water jugs clunked together. A police officer looked in my direction, and then draped a white sheet over the man's body. I loaded the empty bottles into my Jeep and went home.

10

IT FELT AS IF the living room was squeezing against my body, like a boa constrictor wrapped around prey, increasing its grip with each exhale.

Gas, gas, gas.

I pulled a gas mask from its case, slammed it against my face, and then stretched its thick rubber straps over my head. Hand to filter, suck in: The seal of the mask tightened. I grabbed a camouflage Saratoga Suit from the living room floor and slid it over my clothing. MOPP level four. Nothing was exposed. Rubber gloves clung to my sweaty hands. Vinyl booties covered tan desert boots. The Saratoga Suit's hood shielded my head and neck. All of that would protect me from being slimed by Saddam but not from being cooked alive by the sun.

I never doubted the need for all the gear: sarin gas, mustard gas, and VX could've made for a bad day in the desert, a bad day anywhere, and Saddam had kept each one at his disposal at some point. That wasn't disputed. The tens of thousands of people, mainly Kurds and Iranians, he'd already covered with the stuff could've vouched for that. Why would we be any different?

While mustard gas probably wouldn't have killed any of us right away, we would've wished we were dead. Imagine massive red welts, pus-filled sores, blindness, and blood oozing from blistered lungs. A horrible way to go, but mustard gas was the least of our NBC (nuclear, biological, chemical) worries, because if there is a devil, he comes in the form of nerve agents like VX or sarin. After defecating and drooling all over our uniforms, we'd most likely twitch on the ground for a few excruciating seconds before falling comatose. That's what we had to look forward to if our charcoal-lined chemical protective clothing or rubber masks failed—and we all knew most of the gear we carried had been manufactured by the lowest bidder. But just in case none of that worked or we didn't get into our gear fast enough, the Department of Defense had also outfitted us with Mark 1 kits—autoinjectors full of the nerve-agent antidotes atropine and 2PAM. Our corpsman, who had received a five-minute class on the kit, gathered the platoon in a circle and told us we would have to slam the needles into the meaty portion of one of our thighs if the occasion arose. You know, once we got done soiling our trousers. Of course, all of that was in addition to the shots, pills, and inoculations we'd already received: a series of anthrax shots that felt like slugs of lead as they were injected into our arms; one smallpox immunization that created dime-sized scabs that may or may not have had the ability to transmit smallpox to whoever touched the circular sore; and a daily dose of malaria pills that made many of the Marines nauseous. If the war didn't kill anybody, we were pretty sure the military medical system would.

The gas mask straps cut into my head. Sand blew in through the air-conditioning vents and clouded my vision. It swept across the living room, created dust devils in the kitchen. I grabbed a fistful of the sand from the floor. It was mine: as much a part of me as the blood that was rushing out of my head, as tangible as my legs. Grinding the enamel off of my teeth, I could feel capillaries expanding while the veins on the side of my forehead pulsed. Blinding light bounced through my retinas, transmitted ghost signals to my brain. "Take a deep breath. Relax," I said to myself. Already waist-high, the sand kept piling higher. I tried to move but the dune had trapped my body. It enveloped me, pressed tight against my chest.

I managed to pull my body out of the mound and walked out into the wasteland that was in my head. One rubber-encased foot in front of the other. Beat, step, beat, step. I jogged to my heart's cadence. It was an eight-minute-a-mile pace. I could tell.

"Clint," a paramedic said. At some point he'd noticed a framed photograph of Sergeant Van Winkle that Sara kept on the coffee table and mentioned that he had also been a Marine and, I believe, he had been talking about his time in the Corps while we sat there waiting for the results of the medical devices he'd attached to me. I wasn't really sure. I had a mission to go on, so I ignored him and kept moving forward. Each step carried me farther away from the living room and the fire trucks and the heart monitor and all the firemen wearing suspenders who must've thought I had been smoking crystal meth. Twenty-eight-year-olds don't usually have heart attacks. "Hey," the paramedic said again. He removed the heart monitor from the end of my index finger and then unwrapped the blood pressure cup from my right biceps. "You checked out okay." He jotted a few notes down. I sank deeper into my chair. Three other Phoenix firefighters broke from watching the Arizona Diamondbacks game to pack up the medical gear and headed out of the front door.

I stood in the carport, watched the fire truck and ambulance pull away. A few of my neighbors were in their front yards, looking toward my house, but acted like they'd just been watering their lawns or taking out the garbage when they noticed I was standing outside. I forced a smile, waved anyway.

The rumbling from the fire truck's diesel engine could still be heard when Sara's white Toyota turned into our driveway.

"Did you see the fire department?" she asked while getting out of her car.

"Yeah, I saw them. They were here."

"Did you catch something on fire?"

"No, it was me . . . thought I was having a heart attack and dialed 911. Must be a slow day in Phoenix because the whole fire station showed up. Bet the neighbors think somebody died over here after a scene like that."

She wrapped her arms around my waist, pressed her face into my neck. I wiggled out of her embrace, took a step back. "I'm all right," I said. "The medic told me everything checked out fine. I'm good to go." I paused for a second, tried to think of something else to say, a way of explaining what had happened, a way of explaining to her something I couldn't explain to myself. It seemed like my body was falling apart, rejecting my memories and experiences.

"It was nothing, really. I'm okay."

"Do you want me to drive you to the VA?"

I shook my head no. What was the point? I'd been to the VA too many times. We both had. We'd grown to know the place well.

I had had a whole host of minor medical issues, and as soon as one problem cleared up, another ailment would surface. A mysterious rash formed on the side of my head a few months after I returned from Iraq, but disappeared before anyone could figure out what it was, or if it was the Baghdad boil that had been showing up on other vets. It itched a little, and looked like a ringworm keg party had taken place above my left ear, but other than that, the puffy rash really wasn't too bad. At least it wasn't as aggravating as the stomach

condition a large percentage of us acquired while living in Diwiniyah.

Fifty-five-gallon oil drums that had been sawed in half and
slid under open-air, wood shelters were supposed to be better
than taking a dump in the desert. But I'd become accustomed
to the wide-open feeling that squatting in the desert afforded
and, personally, preferred it to the new method of straddling
27½ gallons of excrement.

It all started out as a joke. Marines with bandanas wrapped
around their faces gathered around the barrels to stir flaming
waste cocktails with metal engineer stakes they'd scavenged.
They had fun with the detail by dipping their stir sticks into
the barrels and waving half-burnt toilet paper at each other,
happily inhaling the wretched fumes as they attempted to set
each other on fire. But the fun wore off as the lines got longer
and the overflowing barrels got heavier. Eventually, there was
more crap than anyone could handle.

Plumes of the thick, black smoke rode the wind into our
living area. The only thing worse than the smell of the barrels
full of human waste was the smell that came from the barrels
after five gallons of diesel fuel had been dumped into them
and set on fire. After a while we barely noticed the smell, and
the shit-burning detail stopped covering their noses, just
gathered around the barrels and stirred. A handful of Marines
stood in the smoke's path, anxiously waiting for the return of

the red-hot barrels to their positions underneath the circular holes in the plywood.

Private First Class Rickard, who had replaced Bello a few weeks earlier after I shifted crews between vehicles in the section, hovered over Lance Corporal Meyers's gangly body. Meyers hadn't left the back of the track in hours, hadn't gone to morning chow, or even gotten up to use the head.

"Ser-geant," Rickard said, dividing the word into two distinct syllables, pronouncing my rank as two words rather than one. "I don't think Meyers is doing too good."

"Doc is on his way," I said.

"He needs to hurry his happy ass up before ol' skin-and-bones kicks the bucket."

Marines throughout the camp were in the same position as Meyers, and nobody seemed to know what to call the epidemic that had them ruining pairs of PT shorts from losing bouts with diarrhea. Corpsmen called the sickness dysentery; the real doctors, sailors with medical degrees, claimed it was gastroenteritis wreaking havoc on the division; Marines called the episodes Saddam's revenge. It didn't matter what anyone called the sickness, everyone knew what kind of pills they'd be given once they fell victim: 800 mg of Motrin. Doling out piles of the pills seemed to be SOP for the Navy when dealing, medically, with Marines. It was the answer to every medical question, the pill that cured everything. Break an arm? Motrin. Massive head wound? Motrin.

"How about you let me be the sergeant today and you can

be the PFC. Is that okay with you?" I said to Rickard, half expecting the same kind of reply I had given to Gunny after he'd directed the same used-up statement at me.

"Yes, Ser-geant."

"And don't screw with Doc when he gets here."

Doc walked onto the track and knelt down beside Meyers. He hung an IV bag on a cargo hatch latch, rubbed an alcohol swab over a portion of Meyers's right arm, and then unwrapped a syringe. Inching the hollow needle closer toward Meyers's pasty skin, he stopped, adjusted position.

"Do you know how to use that thing?" Rickard asked.

"Bend over and find out," Doc replied. He waved the needle at Rickard, faking a jab at his crotch. "You just wait. It'll be your turn soon and I am going to make sure you pay."

"Fucking sailor," Rickard said as he stepped away from the needle.

"You two have got to be kidding me," I said.

Rickard fell out the very next day, lay in the same place Meyers had been sprawled out. As much as Doc may have wanted revenge, he held back, and gave Rickard an IV, too. I wasn't quite as lucky when I succumbed to the revenge; the division's stash of IVs had been depleted.

I had a two-man tent that didn't exactly belong to me. I had given similar tents to Gunny, Paxson, and Kipper. None of the tents belonged to them either. At least not when the war began. We hadn't stolen them, but we knew who they had been issued to originally. Black letters stenciled on the bottom of my tent read "LT Frank." He wasn't anywhere in sight, though, probably not even in the country anymore, so we utilized his tents in lieu of his presence. He was a good guy, and usually thorough, but had slipped up and left his platoon's tents in the AAV when we parted ways. He should've kept a better eye on his platoon's stuff because, everyone knows, "Gear adrift is a gift."

The tents trapped the heat. Just made you sweat more. The inside of mine smelled like underarms, dirty feet, and Purell hand sanitizer. A half-inch of dirt covered the floor and every move I made created a nails-on-the-blackboard sound as the dirt scratched against the nylon floor. None of that mattered. Privacy was at a premium and we'd all become accustomed to discomfort. So, when the sickness hit me, I crawled into my little cave and slept through the 120-degree days, the stench of the multiple shit-burning sessions, and the noise coming from the world outside the tent.

My body felt like an AAV had stopped on top of my chest and pivoted there. A crust had formed around my mouth; sticky matter clumped in the corners of my eyes. Gurgling noises originating in my stomach were worrisome, and I prayed I wouldn't end up like many of the Marines, who had involuntarily released the contents of their intestines into their PT shorts. Kipper unzipped the tent and poked his head inside. "You have to stay hydrated," he said. He extended a canteen.

"Okay," I wheezed while reaching for it.

Paxson walked onto the back of my amtrac the next day. "Did you shit yourself?" he asked. It had become a legitimate question around the camp. I shut my war journal and stowed it in the back of my flak jacket.

"No, but my ass is raw." I paused for a moment. "Am I losing my mind? Swore I heard a trombone, or something, this morning."

"It's the fucking band," he said.

"The band. What band?"

"First Division Band. They've been at it since yesterday morning."

"Unbelievable."

"Tell me about it. Couldn't hardly believe my ears either, but then I walked over there and got a look. Craziest fucking thing I'd ever seen. Flutes, tubas, clarinets, and shit. Practicing like they're back on the block."

"Want to get Kipper and go mess with them?" I asked.

"Naw, man, we can't. Some fools got caught chucking rocks at them. So now there's a standing order to leave them alone. Shit-ass Kipper is sick anyway. Sweating it out in his tent."

We walked over to Kipper's tent, unzipped it, and poked our heads in. He was curled up like a baby, holding his belly. We mixed grape Powerade in his canteens, encouraged him to take a drink, and then headed for the music without him.

Years later, the effects of Saddam's revenge still lingered in our guts. That, coupled with the mysterious rashes and anger issues, kept me in the VA enough. I'd been herded from clinic to clinic. Poked and prodded by various devices, I had seen more than my fair share of VA doctors. I certainly didn't want to go back to that hospital if I could help it.

Sara wrapped her arms around my waist again.

"I'll put my stuff in the house and take you to the VA," she said.

"Not today. I've got another appointment next week. I can make it until then. Honestly, don't worry about me. I'll be fine. Go inside, relax a bit."

I don't know how many times after that incident I rushed to the VA thinking I was having a heart attack, thinking I'd finally made it to the end of the line. Maybe six or eight times. Maybe more. Sara would drive me to the VA and we would sit in the emergency room and wait. Each time, I ended up going home without medication, a diagnosis, or even an explanation of what was taking place. All I was told was that my blood pressure was fine and that I was too young to have a heart attack. It wasn't until a few months after the fire department incident that an urgent-care nurse bothered to give an explanation, telling me that I was having panic attacks and that I didn't need to keep showing up at the VA in the middle of the night every other week.

One more symptom to add to my crazy list.

For some reason my mind had been putting my body into fight-or-flight mode when there wasn't any danger present. All of it was just in my head. I knew that. Still, the episodes continued, for no apparent reason, hitting me like a runaway locomotive, leaving nothing but unidentifiable pieces of flesh in its wake. But the attacks only came when I was sober. So I started to drink even more. My head became a fuming barrel of waste. The sludge needed to be burnt and dumped.

Storm clouds appeared from behind the cacti-dotted mountains. Swaying mesquite and paloverde trees released their leaves into the road. A gust of wind wrapped the sun-bleached American flag around its pole. Fat raindrops splattered onto the cement. I reached up and attempted to fix the flag, then went inside to my office.

Twisted beer cans overflowed the garbage can. I rubbed a hand over my unshaven face and opened the death journal. JJ DID TIE BUCKLE was scribbled inside the front cover. It is an acronym for the fourteen Marine Corps leadership traits: Justice, Judgment, Dependability, Initiative, Decisiveness, Tact, Integrity, Enthusiam, Bearing, Unselfishness, Courage, Knowledge, Loyalty, and Endurance. I learned that as a recruit on Parris Island.

We learned firsthand about other acronyms on the Iraqi battlefield. EPW, KIA, POW, and MIA are the letters that spun around our minds, the alphabet soup we had to deal with while trying to maintain JJ DID TIE BUCKLE during our portion of the war, which had been dubbed OIF 1 (Operation Iraqi Freedom 1). Keeping the leadership traits intact meant more than just being a good leader; they kept other Marines from becoming casualties, and that, to me, was always the most important part of any mission.

I tried hard to retain the Marine Corps leadership traits in civilian life, to maintain some semblance of my former self. I would have accepted being a quarter of the person I had once been, if a sour stomach and mysterious rashes were the only medical issues I had to worry about.

I flipped through the death journal's sand-laced pages, inhaled every single particle that floated off them. Sergeant Van Winkle's voice came up from the pages. "Keep going," he ordered. "Keep flipping through." I stopped at the entry dated 14 April 2003. "Good place to start," he said. I read the solitary page.

We were already awake and readying ourselves for a patrol when the loudspeakers perched atop the minarets sent the morning *adhan* into the city. On really good days, we'd get to go out on patrol right after the first call to prayer and before the energy-draining heat took hold. But we weren't *that* lucky on the fourteenth. Instead, we lingered around the warehouse compound the entire morning, then headed out during the hottest part of the day. The patrol wasn't too bad. We raided one of Saddam's bunkers (unfortunately, he wasn't home) and kicked in a few doors on our way out of the neighborhood. I didn't have any reason to be pissed off. Everything went smoothly, nobody got hurt, and only a few people shot at us. By the time the call to prayer echoed through the warehouse complex for the final time that day, I'd already put in a full day's work and was standing naked underneath a five-gallon camping shower, washing away a month's accumulation of dirt, which I found to be pretty impressive—not the shower part, but that I'd gone an entire month since my last one.

The war was different then. There weren't any e-mails or televisions or video games. No hot chow or USO shows. So, even a cold shower should've made the rest of the week seem rosy. But I'd read the journal before, hell, lived it, so I knew what to expect.

"Now what?" I asked.

"Don't puss out on me. We're gonna get knee-deep into this shit. Next page. Forward march," said the sergeant.

I turned the page. The pen strokes after the fourteenth of April looked like another person had written them. A peculiar, almost evil, energy radiated from the page. Something had changed in me within a twenty-four-hour time frame. At some point, and for some unknown reason, the "B" had broken off and left me with just an "UCKLE." Bearing had slipped out of the building. It happened that fast, crept up like a sandstorm. If I had to guess, that's where it all started, where I began to transition acronyms. It was the end of the dream and beginning of the nightmare. While I couldn't pinpoint what had caused my downward spiral, I knew approximately when it began. Not much of a consolation prize, but better than nothing.

Losing your mind is a personal issue not many talk about. I think Kipper's nightmare began a few weeks before mine, although I'm not entirely sure. Still, looking back, it seems likely.

At the time, most of the Marines in our platoon were talking about a lance corporal who'd been medevacked out of the area after he had managed to cut a few fingers off in a noncombat-related incident. According to the rumor, he'd been grinning like a schoolboy as they loaded him into the chopper because even though he'd forever have to use his toes if he wanted to count to ten, he was leaving Iraq for good. The joke that evolved from the rumor went something like this: He probably would've thrown the V sign in the air when the helicopter lifted off but only had enough fingers to display a "hang loose." He'd left his peace fingers in the back of an AAV.

It was halfhearted joking at best, comic relief that didn't relieve anything. It didn't seem like anybody could shake the feeling that Al Kut, the next stop on our sightseeing tour through Mesopotamia, might be the final destination for many of us. Death could've happened anywhere, sure, but the hype surrounding that particular city gave everyone an uneasy feeling and led some, like that lance corporal, to carelessness.

I coated the guts of my weapons with lube, scrubbed their metal parts with an all-purpose brush, and wiped them clean. Kipper climbed to the top of my vehicle, squatted beside the turret. I kept scrubbing. If I was going to die, it wasn't going to be because of dirty weapons.

"Sergeant Van Winkle," he said.

"What?"

"I fucked up."

"As long as you didn't lose your rifle, it can be fixed," I yelled up to him.

That was true. Losing a weapon was an unforgivable sin,

especially for a noncommissioned officer. Just about everything else could be worked through.

"I tried to kill him," he said.

"Wait one!" I yelled. "I'm coming up there."

I wiggled from behind the weapons, pulled myself out of the turret and onto the top of the AAV. Kipper sighed loudly, turned his bright red face away from me.

"I couldn't take it anymore. His fucking mouth. His voice. The way he says shit for no reason at all," Kipper said.

"Look at me," I said. "Who are you talking about? Camacci?"

Sergeant Camacci wasn't a bad guy, but had been riding Kipper's ass from the very beginning. He rode everybody's ass. He was that kind of sergeant. Not bad, just loud, and often obnoxious to lower-ranking marines. As a corporal, Kipper had to endure Camacci's tirades when I only had to tell the small-framed sergeant to pipe down.

"Uh-huh. He said some shit that rubbed me wrong, so I reached up into the turret and grabbed him. I tried to yank his pistol out of his holster but couldn't get it out. He was that close to getting it," he said. "I really fucked up this time."

"Jesus, Kip. You can't be doing that kind of shit. C'mon, of all people, *you* know better than to pull a stupid fucking stunt like that. We're Marine NCOs. We've got to maintain our bearing."

Kipper took it for as long as he could. He listened, obeyed orders, and put up with all the nonsense until something finally broke inside him. While I couldn't condone his action,

I couldn't blame him either. Every man has a breaking point. I just hoped it was possible to return once that point had been reached.

I closed the journal, leaned back in the chair, and thought about the pages I'd just read. For the first time, I realized that I might not be alone in my battle. Was it possible that millions of other vets were going through the exact same thing? I couldn't be the only one. Right? But nobody talks about the mental wounds. It is the unseen injury that slips through the cracks, leads people to drinking, puts pressure on spouses, and causes healthy men to call the fire department for ghost symptoms. You are supposed to about-face and forward-march, forget about the war as soon as you get home, take 800 mg of Motrin and carry on like nothing ever happened. But how was I supposed to let go when I was reliving it every day?

11

A BOX OF MARLBORO Lights and a twelve-pack of Coronas kept me company. I squeezed the cordless phone between my shoulder and ear, lit a cigarette off one that was still burning. Inhaled. Exhaled. Watched white smoke rings disappear into the darkness. The lawn chair I was sitting in creaked when I reached down for another beer. Empty bottles outnumbered the full ones and were covered and aligned in formation.

Paxson was a couple of thousand miles away at the Norfolk VFW. He went there for the three-dollar pitchers and dollar hotdogs. To get his "swerve on," he would say. The

VFW bar is where you go when you want to get drunk. It is the business end of drinking. No frills, just old-timers and cheap beer. Earlier that day, his friend had been killed in Iraq, along with thirteen other U.S. Marines. Their amtrac had been blown apart by a roadside bomb, tossed end over end by the massive explosion. Pieces of the fourteen men were still scattered about the area, waiting to be found so they could be boxed up and shipped home.

Call-waiting beeped. I juggled the phone, cigarette, and beer to answer the incoming call. It was Kipper. His friend was dead, too. Nobody else understood.

"Bout time, shit-ass," Paxson said when I clicked back over to him. He was downing his third pitcher of beer and starting to slur his words. I let him talk; took drags off my cigarette and guzzled a lukewarm beer. "I'm going to get his name tattooed on my forearm," he added. "I am going back to Iraq. I am going to kill some more of those motherfuckers. Brad's dead. I'm going to kill those raghead motherfuckers, all of them. Just like before. Fuck them. Fuck them all."

The stagnant heat of August, silhouettes of palm trees against a waning moon, and dust devils reminded me of the place I was trying to forget, the place where those Marines had lost their lives. A police helicopter that had been buzzing over my house only enhanced the feeling. If only I could've felt the heat of an explosion or had a few dozen bullets crash through the plate glass window, then everything would've been perfect. I could've low-crawled to the alley and returned fire. Opened up and let the neighborhood have it.

———

Paxson and Kipper were sitting in lawn chairs behind Gunny Yates's AAV. Gunny Donahoo, Staff Sergeant Beck, and Gunny sat across from them, with their feet propped up on MRE boxes. "Grandma's House" was the name we gave Gunny Yates's AAV. It was a retreat from the troops, a place full of goodies. When not patrolling, Gunny would lower the ramp of his AAV halfway and make his crewmen set the chairs out in a semicircle around the vehicle's field-expedient coffee table. Hanging out with a gunnery sergeant, especially Gunny Yates, was dangerous for a sergeant. The threat of being volunteered (voluntold) for working parties always loomed. However, Gunny Yates was good company and often entertaining. We took our chances. The playful bantering and conversations were cleansing. Away from our troops, we were able to unwind and enjoy the fact that we'd made it through the war as long as we had. And even though the crackling of automatic weapons and the roar of explosions were constantly within earshot, we were able to find relief from the war while sitting in those plastic lawn chairs, sharing everything we had.

We shared chow, jalapeño cheese spread from our MREs, and confiscated candy. We passed around war souvenirs, Iraqi weapons, and rumors. We even shared chewing tobacco. When the chewing tobacco ran out, we switched to cigarettes, which were just as scarce as chew until our sister unit liberated a cigarette factory and Paxson showed up, like the Pied Piper of tobacco, with a massive cardboard box filled to the brim with

141

packs of an Iraqi brand of cigarettes called Sumar. Just about everyone began to smoke and most left Iraq with a pack-a-day habit and a hankering for the gritty taste of third-world cigs.

My hands were calloused and stained. They smelled like diesel fuel, beef ravioli, wintergreen chewing tobacco, and gunpowder. However, that didn't stop me from cramming my fingers into my mouth whenever chewing tobacco was available. My boots and feet were in a worse condition and could've been the weapons of mass destruction everyone was talking about but couldn't seem to find. Nobody noticed, though, because we all stank in our unwashed uniforms, which had stains on the stains. Pax pulled a handful of baby wipes from a Ziploc bag and tossed the package over to me. I yanked a fistful out, handed a few to Kipper, and then scrubbed the sludge from between my toes, used a new wipe to wash away the mud-packed creases that cut across my face like a series of dried-up desert rivers.

"Got smokes?" Kipper asked Pax.

Paxson threw a dirty baby wipe at him, walked inside the vehicle to find the pack of Sumar cigarettes he'd seen Dona-hoo stash in the pamphlet box. He rooted around for the blue package. Kipper snuck up behind him, reared his hand back. The sound of his cupped hand violating Paxson's ass echoed through the AAV.

"Good game," Kipper yelled.

Paxson rubbed his backside through his olive drab Nomex jumpsuit. The rest of us cheered like the home team had just scored a touchdown.

"All right, shit piece. Game on," Pax said.

It was a game we'd been playing for years. We mocked base-ball players and the friendly ass pats they give each other after they hit a home run or catch a pop fly. However, we'd taken it a step farther and often ended up with handprints emblazoned on our backsides. The welts made our wives and girlfriends curious, probably scared. But eventually the women caught on: It was just another one of the childish games Marines play. They knew what to expect.

Back in the rear, before the war, we always played games. Our games weren't family friendly and usually involved embarrassing, defiling, or insulting another Marine. The best one was the shitter game, which really wasn't much of a game for the guy who was sitting on the toilet. Once the mark was seated in the maintenance bay head, one of us would quietly open the door as another Marine hurried out to the ramp, turned the fire hydrant on, and then pulled the attached hose next to the stall. Pax and I had it down to a science and were able to pull it off effortlessly, drenching our victims before they knew what had hit them or had time to escape. The best part was that the force from the water gushing out of the fire hose was strong enough to pin the seated Marine to the toilet. He would flounder. We would yell at him.

Except for the occasional "good game" ass slap or "foul ball" crotch shot, we didn't have time to play many games in Iraq. But we managed to squeeze them in.

Paxson found the smokes, returned to his lawn chair. Kipper couldn't stop laughing. He rocked back and forth, pointing and laughing, his face flushed with delight. He seemed amused by the game, amused that he was alive, amused that we were all alive.

"How'd that feel, boy?" he managed.

In between his snorting and laughing, I heard a faint thud. It was really nothing, merely sounded like a person had flicked a piece of cardboard, and the sound might have gone unnoticed if we had been anywhere else. Kipper straightened up, became serious. I looked around, tried to locate the source of the noise. Kipper was staring at something. I followed his eyes with mine. Kipper's flak jacket was a few inches away from him, lying on the AAV's ramp, with his helmet upside down on top of it. A stray round had weaved its way through the crowd and landed atop Kipper's flak jacket. It spun momentarily. He picked it up and showed it to the rest of us. Nobody said anything. Then Kipper started laughing again. He laughed harder than he had before; he laughed and lit up a smoke. The rest of us reached for cigarettes, lit up, and laughed with him.

Somewhere in there, in between the friendship and ass-slapping games, Kipper had dodged his bullet. He had persuaded it to spin by him, by us, and afterward all we could do was laugh about the goddamned bullet that was supposed to rip into Kipper. The laughter ended, though—blew out with the last Iraqi sandstorm that had ravaged us years before. We became separated: Kipper was home with his wife in North Carolina, Paxson was at the Norfolk VFW with his three-dollar pitchers, and I was on my back porch with my smokes and the Arizona heat. Still, all by ourselves, we had each other.

And that day, that day when a fellow Marine hadn't been as lucky, we sat around thinking about how bad things could've been and how much we were going to miss him.

Although I'd never known Brad, I missed him, too. I missed him because he represented something. He was one of us, a United States Marine, a Marine who had been knocked off the shitter by the water hose or who had hobbled onto the back of an AAV after getting flicked in the balls.

He should've been home, drinking a beer, talking about the war with his buddies.

Countless hours of long-distance phone calls and too many unshakable memories kept us together. We'd deal with our private wars for weeks, even months, before calling to unload. We were each other's therapists and retold the same stories over and over again as if we were trying to convince ourselves of something, trying to convince each other that it was okay and that it was all just a game. Even though we came home with big red welts on our asses, reminders to our wives that we were just out playing childish games—games with guns, dead babies, stray bullets, and rattled minds—maybe, just maybe, it was a good game after all. A game we won because we lived through it.

I wished I could've found a way to soak it all up and take the burden and pain away from my mourning friends, to find a few magic words to comfort them. But there isn't anything you can say to guys who have just lost a friend in combat, that much I did know. Nothing would make everything better. I couldn't resurrect their friend or erase their memories. The dead would still be dead no matter what anyone did. So I quietly continued to sip my beer and smoke my cigarettes, listened and hoped that things would eventually pan out for all of us, and that we would be lucky enough to dodge the next round of bullets.

There were Marines in Iraq who had been just as close to the men who'd been killed, but war doesn't stop because of death, and those Marines had geared up, gotten back in their tracks, and ventured into the belly of the beast even though they were a few men short. When stuff like that happens, you have to push it into the back of your mind and keep rolling. There'll be plenty of time to think about it all when you get home.

"Hold on," I told Pax.

I clicked back over to Kipper.

"About goddamn time," Kipper yelled into the phone.

"Wait one. Dave is on the other line. I'll call you back on three-way," I said.

I was still at a loss for words but had to find a way to break through the silence. All I could think about was Iraq and how lucky we'd been, so I mentioned the bullet incident in Baghdad.

"It happened at Paxson's vehicle, not Gunny's," Kipper said after I finished telling my version of the story.

"We were in the junkyard, not at the shit hole warehouse place," Paxson added.

"Are you sure?" I asked.

"Positive," Kipper said. "Donahoo, Beck, and Yates weren't there either. It was Brannon, Braudis, and Sheridan. And you were on patrol."

Was I on patrol? I took another swig of warm beer, lit another cigarette, and thought about what they'd just told me. They were right. I hadn't been there. I was walking by a playground in Saddam City. I remember the gravel crunching under my boots. A group of Iraqi boys were playing soccer with a ball they'd made by wrapping duct tape around a shirt. I walked forward, with my head turned, watching the boys kick the ball around the dirt lot. A barefoot boy kicked the soccer ball past the goalkeeper. "Stop!" yelled a grunt. I froze, moved my attention toward the voice. He pointed down at my boot, which was still suspended in the air. A little white streamer waved from a gray cylinder that was poking out of a clump of dirt. "Cluster bomb," he continued. It looked like a spent 40 mm casing to me and not like any bomb I'd ever seen. I pulled my foot back and placed it on the deck behind me. I could've sworn I heard birds chirping even though we were standing in the middle of an empty field.

"That was close," the grunt said.

"Good game," I replied.

"What'd you say?" Paxson asked over the phone.

"Nothing, I'm just a little confused," I said.

12

It HAD ONLY BEEN a few weeks since Brad's death, but it seemed like it had just happened. His death had been hard on the entire unit, especially Paxson, who had been sent to escort his buddy's flag-draped casket home from Dover Air Force Base and then participated in the funeral. He never said it was rough, but I could sense that it was probably the toughest duty he'd ever done. It had to be. What he did say about the episode is private, but it imprinted a mental image I've never been able to shake.

Instead of humping a pack through the sand, where I probably belonged, I was banging away on a keyboard at a twenty-four-hour café that catered to the insomniacs, hippies, and freaks of Phoenix. Being two of the three, I should've fit right in. But I didn't.

An abstract painting of Osama bin Laden hung on the wall, and he watched over my shoulder through the thick, lung-clogging cigarette smoke. He looked friendly in the painting, smiling at the coffee-drinking crowd. Nobody else gave him a second look.

Damn, I thought. This is too perfect to be true—I couldn't make this kind of shit up.

It was two A.M. but there were plenty of hippies hanging out with Osama and me: smoking, drinking coffee, and working on a variety of messed-up ideas while a long-haired fat man played CDs over a booming sound system. I wondered if they were mocking me because the teeth-grinding rave tunes that had been playing gave way to John Lennon.

"All we are saying is give peace a chance."

Were they trying to tell me something? Had they caught a glimpse of the Marine emblem I displayed on the back of my vehicle? Things just got stranger and stranger, which was situation normal for me, especially since I'd been home.

While I wanted to buy into that whole peace vibe and really give it a chance, I couldn't help but think of those dead Marines and the thousands of other Americans who were sent to die for a so-called Iraqi freedom. I was stuck somewhere between wanting to take Lennon's advice and wanting to man a machine gun. Where the fuck did I fit in?

Osama smiled, Lennon crooned, the artsy types stared.

The coffee-guzzling hippies couldn't stop talking about San Francisco and how great that land of liberal living was, while squads of Marines, thousands of miles away, were preparing for another patrol. It was difficult—difficult being mentally stuck somewhere and physically stuck somewhere else, wanting to be in both places at the same time but not wanting to believe in either. Their hearts were stuck in San Fran; mine was somewhere in Iraq.

Kuwait. Gunny Yates held up a propaganda rag. It was a U.S. government publication, or something equally objective, a real pillar of the journalism community. The large picture on the front page took up half the space above the fold, and showed a group of Americans burning the American flag—the same one we were about to be sent to fight under. We gathered around, gawked at the spectacle in disbelief.

Anytime Gunny got ahold of something, the entire tent noticed. He always seemed to have the most up-to-date information about our forthcoming war. Plus, he had commandeered a shortwave radio, and had it hanging from the tent pole next to his living space. The jingle that preceded the BBC news silenced the entire tent every time, partly because we had gotten used to Gunny Yates yelling, "Lock your goddamn mouths," at us whenever the British voice began to report on world affairs. So we were always looking in that direction, waiting for a Brit to break through the noise. It wasn't like we had anything else to do.

"Goddamned tree huggers," said a young lance corporal who was standing in front of me. He rocked back and forth on his heels. Shook his head from side to side.

Even though I wasn't clear on the reasons behind the invasion of Iraq, nor did I really care, I did know it wasn't my decision. "Marines don't pick their wars, just fight in them" is a common saying. If Americans hadn't wanted us over there, then they probably should've opened their mouths a few months before we were staged and ready to go. The government spent millions of dollars getting all of us into the Kuwaiti desert, and I was pretty sure that burning a couple of flags wasn't going to change anything. Anyway, I had really hoped it wouldn't. Fuck them and the United Nations. I wanted to blow some shit up.

The flag burners in the picture had pissed off everyone in the tent. Marines cycled through to see the picture, to offer their comments of disdain. Kipper said he would've punched the people in the face had he been present and claimed he would hunt them down once we got home. Several Marines mentioned the parallel between our fighting and their freedom to burn the flag. The catchphrase "Freedom isn't free" was thrown around liberally, even though it didn't apply to the situation. Marines shook their heads, kicked the ground, flipped off the picture, complained to their buddies, and vowed to avenge the fiery piece of cloth.

"O say, can you see . . . "

———

I wondered if any of those San Francisco daydreamers sitting around the coffee shop were the ones in the picture, burning the flag, and if they knew a Marine combat vet had infiltrated their hangout. I wanted to burn a rainbow-colored, tie-dyed T-shirt for all of my irate Marines, for the handful of men who'd eaten the big one that day. Still, I wasn't sure I wanted to take sides anymore. I wanted to be able to blend in some-where, to camouflage myself into the civilian world, and just watch stuff happen without getting ticked off.

There wasn't anything for me to blow up. Nobody in Phoenix needed me to shoot them, needed me to roll through their neighborhood, set their house on fire, or liberate them. Nope, none of that, just grinning Osama, iced espresso, and a gaggle of freaks.

"Every silver lining has got a touch of gray," wailed Jerry Garcia over the café's sound system.

It wasn't the first time I'd been surrounded by the peace crowd. Fourteen months prior I'd gone to the Tempe presi-dential debate between President George W. Bush and Sena-tor John Kerry. I'd managed to weasel my way into press passes and was fully credentialed even though I didn't have any business being credentialed for anything, much less an event as important as the debate. Still, I'd received clearance to attend and was given a press pass complete with the Secret Service hologram logo on the front.

Liberals, conservatives, hippies, and Jesus freaks swarmed

the grounds of Arizona State University's main campus, lingered outside a gated area where important press people like me were going to congregate later that evening. Political parties, some I'd never heard of, pleaded their cases to whoever would listen. Packs of reporters moved through the crowds with cameras, microphones, laptops, and agendas. It seemed like anyone who cared about anything had turned up to try to change the world and to persuade others to sign on with their harebrained organizations. Political parties wanted votes, corporations were looking for college-aged customers, and the Christians just wanted a few souls. I couldn't find anything I was looking for.

Thousands of white crosses jutted out of a lush green lawn. Each memorial represented an American who had been killed in Iraq or Afghanistan. I walked through the rows and columns, watched the passing crowd. A few people stopped, but most acted as if they had better things to do and barely gave the pseudo graveyard a second look. I kneeled in front of a cross, rubbed my hands over the wood. Everything went silent. The crowds of people disappeared. I reached into my backpack and pulled out a flask. "Here's to us," I said to the cross before unscrewing the top and taking a swing of rum.

When I looked up, the crosses were gone. People had taken their places and were standing at the position of attention in front of them. Their tan and brown camouflage uniforms contrasted against the bright green grass. I rubbed my eyes. Took another swig.

"Glad you could make it," a voice said.

"We looked for you," I replied.

"I know you did. Don't sweat it, really. If it makes you feel any better, another unit got me, eventually." He paused. "Looks like you're at it again."

"What, drinking?"

"No, dwelling. Letting your mind drift."

Gunny Yates's voice filtered in over the platoon frequency. I reached up to my comm helmet and flipped the switch to answer him.

"This is Stinky," I replied. "Send it."

"Get your binos to your face."

"Roger that."

"Look to your two o'clock," Gunny ordered. I traversed the turret in that direction, pressed the binoculars against my face. Four or five straggly dogs were gathered near a telephone pole, jockeying for position around an object I couldn't identify.

"Do you see the dogs?" he asked.

"Roger, I've got eyes on the dogs."

"What the fuck are they eating?"

The dogs had been gnawing at something, but I couldn't tell what it was or figure out why Gunny cared so much about what Iraqi mutts ate for dinner. I moved the binoculars in Gunny's direction. He was halfway out of his turret, staring at the dogs through his own pair of binoculars. "Goddammit, Stinky," he yelled over the radio. "Is it a person?" I started to think about the operation brief the CO had given before we moved into Shatra. An American soldier had disappeared. He was presumed dead, but if we happened upon his body, we were supposed to load him into the back of an amtrac. It sounded all too familiar.

My gut tightened, neck stiffened. "Jesus Christ," I said to myself, "this can't be happening." The idea that it might have been a person bothered me just as much as if it had been one. I had seen a lot of gruesome things, but nothing could've prepared me for seeing a body being eaten like a pile of trash. We'd already left one dead American behind, in Nasiriyah, and I certainly didn't want to do that all over again.

I lowered myself into the turret, sighted in on the pack of dogs. I had them in my crosshairs and was ready to press the .50-cal's butterfly trigger. A blast from deep within the city rattled my vehicle. My head bobbed forward, knocked my eye into the sight. No damage. I regained my composure, sighted in on the dogs again, and continued to watch them until it was time to leave.

I snuck another swig from my flask. The memorial I had chosen to drink beside could've been for anyone, since none of the wooden crosses had names inscribed on them. "Was that you?" I asked the cross. I rubbed my hand over its surface again, then stood up and walked away.

Quakers manned a table a few hundred yards away from the cemetery and, strangely enough, across the sidewalk from a Marine recruiter's traveling motivation station. Posters of Marines jumping from planes, bumper stickers with catchy slogans, and a pull-up bar challenge were set up, but getting little action from the college crowd. A multitude of antiwar literature was littered across the Quakers' table, alongside a book they had filled with photos of all the American service members who had been killed in Iraq and Afghanistan. I wanted to study the faces in the book but somebody was already flipping through its pages, casually, like it was a Sears catalog and he was shopping for a riding lawnmower or electric pencil sharpener. The man noticed the faded blue U.S. Marines ball cap I was wearing and moved away.

I took my time with the pictures. None of the people at the table said anything to me, which was probably the best thing for all of us. Even though I didn't have a problem with their stance on the war, and was even beginning to understand it, a little, I wasn't in the mood to hear about the war from somebody who hadn't been there. I just wanted to look at their book, see the photos of the dead troops.

I stopped at a picture of a Marine amtracker who had died in Nasiriyah. I didn't know him, but Gunny had, and I recognized his name. I'd seen his smoldering deathbed firsthand. I stared at his picture, mumbled something about Nasiriyah, and then walked away.

A few feet away from the table a female student pressed a flyer into my hand and started rambling on about the "small nuclear bombs" that were being used in Iraq. "Slap rounds?" I questioned. She didn't answer. Her scruffy counterpart, who had been sitting cross-legged on the ground, smashed a lit cigarette into the dirt and walked closer.

"No. You know, they are using these little nuclearlike bullets on the battlefields, like everywhere. Troops are getting supersick from the stuff. People are dying. It's crazy-scary, like a mini nuke war," he said.

"You're talking about slap rounds," I said again. "But you've got your facts twisted. They're depleted uranium, armor-piercing bullets and you'd have to eat them to get sick. Or shove one in your ass. Would you do either?"

"So you've heard of them then?"

Everyone acted like they knew so much about the war. But none of them really knew anything besides what they had learned through Internet searches or shady half-truths political pundits spouted from the comfort of their news desks. Nothing could ever be flushed out because nobody bothered to ask the troops or look at both sides of the story. You could either be a nuke-the-world conservative or a hug-'em-all liberal. No middle ground seemed to exist. Either way, the troops who had been there, the few people who knew exactly what a slap round and smoldering amphibious assault vehicle looked like, were ignored. Only the Marine recruiter, who had a combat-action ribbon pinned to his khaki shirt, and I were even close to the real story. And if he was like me, he probably hadn't been able to pinpoint anything yet either.

I moved across the sidewalk, a few feet away from the recruiter's setup, and catty-corner from the Quaker table. A man in his early twenties passed by carrying a U.S. flag. It had phrases scribbled into its white stripes, dollar signs drawn over the stars, and corporate logos in between. He stopped in front of me, smiled, and turned the flag toward my face.

"Why don't you show your flag to the Marine over there?" I said, pointing to the recruiter's table.

"Huh?"

"Whatever. Go fuck yourself," Sergeant Van Winkle said.

It might've seemed overly patriotic to have gotten so stirred up over a piece of cloth, but that cloth meant something to me. I didn't give a shit about terrorism or Saddam Hussein or Al Qaeda. I didn't care about anybody else's freedom or liberty. I never heard any of that mentioned, and certainly never heard anybody say, "We have to fight these guys here so we don't have to fight them at home." We could've cared less about all of that. The reason we did the things we did were much simpler. We fought for each other. None of the other rah-rah BS mattered. And so when I saw that flag with the scribbling on it, all I could think about were those crosses and how each one represented an American who had died because of that flag. Right or wrong, I didn't want their memories cheapened by a guy who didn't have the cojones to join the military. If the guy was looking for trouble, he'd run smack-dab into it. I didn't have anything to lose.

Static chirped through a set of cheap speakers as Christian music echoed off the buildings' walls, floated back into an alcove.

Just a few more weary days and then,
I'll fly away;

159

Sergeant Van Winkle stared at the flag bearer, prepared to break the guy's neck. The sergeant, I was relatively confident, could have ended that student's life without even breaking a sweat. We had the anger and the training. "He isn't worth it, man," I heard Kipper saying. "He isn't worth it at all." Sergeant Van Winkle did an about-face and marched away, left the guy standing in the middle of the crowd.

Four shots of dark espresso, whole milk, and chocolate syrup dumped over ice was the closest thing I'd found to Gunny Donahoo's Big Sissy. Civilians called it an iced mocha. If only Gunny Donahoo could've acquired ice as easily as Gunny Yates had acquired that sick-looking chicken, we could have kicked back in our plastic lawn chairs and sipped on iced coffee drinks as we watched the fireworks display the Iraqis produced for us each night, wondered how civilians could go through life without ever having to travel to places like Iraq or Afghanistan or Kosovo or Bosnia: places where things needed to be blown up in order to give peace a chance.

There weren't any more wartime coffee concoctions or faulty Intel briefs or Marines to sit and banter with. Instead, I had mochas, CNN, and hippies to keep me company. No more F-bomb dropping whenever needed or ass-chewing sessions. Just five-dollar words and friendly conversation. I could've changed all of that. I could've stopped being a pussy writer and gone back to the Corps, traded in my prose and returned to the rifle. But I couldn't find the nerve to do it all again and couldn't find the nerve to refute any of it—the Marines, the hippies, or the war.

I wasn't sure whether I wanted to give peace a chance or go back to pulling the trigger. The choices seemed so slim, too black and white. Instead, I remained stuck in a world of gray—afraid to make a choice, to remove myself completely from the clatter of the keyboard, or from the pinging of spent brass casings as they dropped onto the turret floor. I hoped there was somewhere between bin Laden and Lennon, somewhere between San Fran and Iraq I would fit in.

I guess I was always looking for something. What it was, I didn't know. I wanted help from the VA, but didn't want to go back, didn't want to be subjected to that second-rate treatment any longer. I wanted to find peace within myself, but didn't know how or where to locate it. I wanted to be a sergeant again, a writer, less angry, a better husband, and to ward off the constant bombardment of war-related thoughts. Most of all, I didn't want any more Americans coming home from Iraq in boxes or with jingle-jangled minds.

13

EASTER SUNDAY 2003 AND all of us were wearing our finest. I had an olive drab fire-retardant jumpsuit on, sleeves rolled twice at the bottom, just high enough to expose the bulging, water-resistant digital watch I had purchased the day before leaving California. The grunts were wearing their usual dingy, old-school desert cammies, complete with butterfly collars that would've made Elvis jealous. Oddly enough, Paxson was all geared up and also planning on attending the warehouse mass. He'd started out as an atheist, but figured it couldn't hurt to believe in something for a few months, at least until the bullets stopped flying. A sentiment felt by many.

Marines searched for whatever it was they thought they

would need to get them through the war. Chaplains baptized men in tubs of water, passed out words of wisdom, and conducted desert services. Even Corporal Hall, who prayed to trees and worshipped the moon, managed to convert a few. The combination of religion and war wasn't unique to our situation. For as long as war has been around, men have fought under the assumption that God was on their side, that *their* Almighty somehow favored *their* bloody cause. Certainly God wanted a U.S. victory in Iraq. At least, I really hoped that was the case. If not, we were all going to pay big-time for the shit we had done.

While in Kuwait, Pax and I decided to wander into the world of religion, a place nearly as foreign to us as the markets in downtown Baghdad. We tromped over to the chaplains' tent, obtained a couple of sets of the ready-made religion packets the chaplains had assembled (little green Bibles, rosary beads, and prayer cards with instructions) and went back to our tent to figure out how to use all of the paraphernalia. Maybe it wasn't the war entirely that led to Pax's new faith, but the fact that both times he impregnated his wife, he had been sent off to war within weeks of finding out. There was, from what I could tell, a direct correlation with Paxson's sperm and war. He'd missed his first son's birth due to Kosovo, and anticipated missing the birth of his second son because of Iraq.

I wasn't sure what the chaplain in the warehouse could tell us that would make us feel better, or what kind of message of love he planned on preaching to the congregation of Marines who had spent the previous month violating several of the Ten Commandments. I did know this: Nobody would be resurrected that day no matter what he said. The Chaplain could say whatever he wanted: No body would rise after three days. Not in Iraq.

The chaplain readied for his flock's arrival anyway. I might not have been Catholic, but Mass was a lot closer to what I knew than the howl-at-the-moon stuff Hall had been peddling. Besides, I'd promised myself, and God, I would go to some kind of religious service. It was, after all, Resurrection Day and I was in the middle of the Holy Land, kind of.

Most of us could've written everything we knew about Iraq on the back of a postcard and still had plenty of room for notes. Nobody bothered to tell us we were in the cradle of civilization or that many people believed the mythical Garden of Eden had been located near Baghdad, somewhere between the Tigris and Euphrates Rivers. If it was there, we trampled through it, kicked the doors in, and shot its citizens. Even if someone had mentioned the importance of some of the places we had ransacked, we probably wouldn't have cared. We might have spent a lot of time drinking those wimpy coffee drinks, but we were United States Marines, not a bunch of milquetoast English lit majors. Unless it had something to do with the U.S. Marines or Americans kicking ass, history and culture didn't appeal to most of us. I could consistently hit a target from five hundred yards away with an M16, execute a blood choke in my sleep, and handle a bayonet like a scalpel. That was all I really needed to know. Right? Knowing about the Tower of Babel or the epic of Gilgamesh wouldn't have changed anything, wouldn't have magically shielded us from shrapnel or bombs. Ignorance is . . .

Sitting on the edge of the turret, waiting for the service to begin, I listened to the grunts in the back of the vehicle talking. "It's Friday night back home; your wives are probably sucking dick," one Marine said to the rest of the squad. Nobody argued. It could have been true, we all knew that, and most likely was true for some.

Marines are realists. Marines are dreamers. The two might seem mutually exclusive, but aren't, especially for Marines in combat. We knew we were going to have to drive into the city each day and take the lives of other human beings and in the process of trying to kill others might also get killed, knew that anything was possible once bullets started to fly and that if we were lucky and didn't get wasted, the guy we had eaten breakfast with a few hours earlier might not be as lucky. We were aware of all of those things yet had to convince ourselves that none of those things would happen, even though everyone knew it was bound to happen to somebody. Still, we had to believe that our luck would hold out and it wouldn't be any of us getting the toe tag, not on that day. We had to believe in something, even though most of us knew better than to believe in anything. All believing did was bring heartache, and no matter how we felt, there was still going to be another patrol. People were still going to die.

It was a tangled knot of contradictions, and when somebody would say something about how your "Suzy" was out messing around with "Jody" (the guy of military lore who goes around stealing the wives and girlfriends of deployed Marines) you'd just shrug your shoulders and tell the other Marine that it didn't matter. "That's life," you'd say. "Your whore of a sister will still be available."

I rested my head against the side of the turret and fell asleep. It was too hot to dream; too many flies were swarming around to be able to get comfortable. The sound track of war hummed. I could feel the sounds as much as hear them: the thunderous booms rattling the tin roofs of the warehouses, the automatic weapons spurting out rounds in not-so-distant battles, and the shattering of windows from the hordes of looters who were roaming the streets. All the noises had implications and wouldn't allow me to fall into a deep sleep. But at least it was some sort of sleep, and, while sleeping, I wasn't in the war totally, but hidden away in a slightly more peaceful part of my mind where wives were faithful and chewing tobacco plentiful.

Lieutenant Frank kicked the bottom of my boot. I looked up.

"Sir," I said.

"We're moving in five mikes."

"Roger that, sir."

Another patrol. Instead of hunting for Easter eggs, we searched for assault rifles, RPGs, and American-made mortar rounds. (There were plenty of weapons to be found. They were everywhere: in schools, abandoned buildings, the sides of roads, and in our hands.) Saddam Hussein took the Easter

Bunny's place and appeared to be as real. I'd seen pictures and been told he was out there, but had little faith that I'd ever catch a glimpse of him in person. Because our unit hadn't been the *very* first American unit to make it into Baghdad, finding Saddam remained our unit's last hope of accomplishing something truly historic—besides the amphibious crossing we'd made into Baghdad, which was, supposedly, the first opposed amphibious landing any U.S. unit had made since the Korean War. That, and finding the stash of WMDs that had gotten us into the war in the first place. Aside from the boxes of sarin gas antidote kits Kipper stumbled upon in an abandoned school, we hadn't seen much of anything. I was pretty sure we had a better chance of catching Saddam, or even seeing the Easter Bunny, than getting our hands on a cache of WMDs. Really, I didn't care either way.

We didn't find Saddam on our patrol, and Easter service had ended by the time we parked our AAVs in the warehouse complex. Pax hadn't gone to church either, had opted to sleep instead.

"No mail today," he said to me as I walked up to his vehicle. "And nobody's got any chew."

"That sucks. Maybe tomorrow something will come in."

"Yeah, fucking right. Shit ain't coming."

"It might," I said.

"Don't hold your breath. Some fat-ass, rear-echelon motherfucker is chewing our tobacco and eating our chow."

"And, don't forget, pounding our women."

Mail was our connection to home. We didn't have anything

to keep us occupied. There weren't any stores we could spend our money in, no way to get ahold of stuff we wanted. We relied solely on the care packages for items of want. But incoming mail was sporadic, at best, and when it didn't arrive, which was usual, we blamed the noncombat types for screwing it up for us. We could never get enough. Every time the big orange, dusty sacks of mail arrived, the Marines were all smiles. No matter how rough the day had been or how many hours we had spent patrolling the streets, dodging bullets, pissing off the locals, and swatting flies, the mail lifted our spirits.

Tobacco, coffee, and porn: the Holy Trinity of combat life and the only things we wanted in our care packages besides letters from our wives or girlfriends. For whatever reason, nobody in the States had enough sense to send much of it. (Sara, especially, refused to send two of the three items.) Instead, the few times we did receive mail, the packages were stuffed full of toilet paper, candy, and baby wipes. There was a mysterious list floating around that had been compiled by someone who wasn't in Iraq and seemed to have thought that we didn't do anything except shit and eat candy all day. Still, each package brought hope. Hope that the parcels would be filled with tobacco, porn, and coffee, with love letters, photographs, and hometown newspaper clippings. Hope that the list master had figured out we had enough toilet paper and sweets. Hope that a perfume-scented letter was stuffed in between the stuff we didn't need and that the women we loved hadn't been out on Friday night.

There were a lot of things to hope for. It was the main

thing that got you through each day. Without it, you didn't have anything. Tobacco, religion, and mail were sources of hope. Drinking Big Sissies and talking with friends were as well. However, peace was never one of them. None of the Marines I knew ever planned on giving peace a chance.

I pinned a combat-action ribbon lapel pin into my faded blue U.S. Marines hat. The white lettering had turned gray. Blue strings dangled from its frayed bill. I'd heard reports of how thousands of wooden crosses, like the ones I'd visited at the Tempe presidential debate, had been erected to coincide with the peace protest being held near downtown Phoenix. But, unlike before, I wouldn't have to guess who the crosses represented. The memorials were supposed to be personalized. They'd have the names of the war dead inscribed on them. I planned on finding a certain cross, rubbing my hands over it, and then placing a Combat Action Ribbon sticker in the middle. It was all planned out. I would do it regardless of what anybody thought about it. I would find the cross that bore the name of Kipper and Paxson's friend and press a decal onto his wooden memorial. I had it all planned.

Cars passing by honked at a line of peaceniks who stood along the busy thoroughfare and crowded into the median. The light turned red. Protesters walked across the road, waved their signs at the stopped cars as they paraded in front. Kumba-fucking-yah, I thought.

I parked, walked to the edge of the event, and positioned

myself next to a line of uniformed police officers. I had intended on applying to the Phoenix Police Department when I first got out of the Marines and even did a ride along with an officer and talked to the recruiter. Form filled out and ready for postage, I changed my mind before sending the application off. I had decided I'd shot about as much as I ever wanted to shoot while in Iraq. I wanted to take it easy, finish school, and then get a job that wouldn't require dodging bullets or dealing with shitty civilians. Plus, I wasn't sure how much control I had left in me, if I could make it through without beating somebody with a nightstick or shooting a person for speeding. Even early on, I was aware that I had some combat-related issues to contend with.

I inched closer to the blue line. I wanted them to notice my hat, to know that I wasn't one of the protesters, that I was different, a Marine vet. Talking heads, most of whom had never seen a day of military service, labeled anybody who objected to the war a traitor. I loved my country so much, especially the men and women in the military, and was afraid of being blackballed for attending a rally, afraid of losing my main support network. But I was also starting to see a trend develop, starting to realize I'd been spending much more time with the granola crowd than the war crowd. Maybe I was giving peace a chance after all.

I finally found the courage to leave the police area and set out on my own, into the unknown world of political activism. At least, I told myself, I wouldn't have to worry about the peace protesters getting violent.

I wandered through the crowd, looked for the traveling cemetery, dodged posters and signs, men yelling through loudspeakers, women carrying American flags. The police filmed the crowd. The crowd filmed the police. I tried to avoid being caught on camera, didn't want to wind up on a national news station, didn't want to become the poster boy for some movement I didn't understand or know much about.

My U.S. Marines hat garnered some attention from a woman who had been walking through the crowd. She sidestepped a man who was holding a sign that said THOU SHALL NOT KILL and made her way toward me. Here we go . . .

"Hello," the young woman said when she got within earshot.

"Hi," I replied, not knowing whether she was trying to pick me up or about to ask a political question. I didn't want to take part in either conversation, but knew that wearing such a hat probably gave the wrong impression, leaving the door wide open.

"An Iraq vet?" she asked.

"Yes, ma'am."

"This war, the whole thing is crap, isn't it? It's heartbreaking how you guys didn't have adequate body armor or the proper types of Hummers," she continued.

Hummers? I tried not to laugh. Soccer moms drive Hummers. Marines operate Humvees.

"We had everything we needed," I replied, hoping the answer would satisfy, rather than intrigue, her. She stood silently, presumably waiting for me to elaborate on the statement. "We had each other. That's all we needed," I said.

I left the protest without finding the field of crosses, the Combat Action Ribbon still in my pocket. I'd gone to try to gain some closure but ended up opening an entirely different can of worms.

I had expected to see people desecrating the flag and hear antitroop slogans being chanted. I expected my U.S. Marines hat might cause trouble and somebody would mouth off to me because of my veteran status. Instead, people were waving American flags and WE SUPPORT THE TROOPS signs at the protest. From what I could gather, the protesters really did support the troops, just not the way they were being used. The realization only made things harder for me. Before, it was "us" against "them." But the protest changed all of that, and I was having a hard time pinpointing who the "them" was. I really wanted to hate the protesters; it would've made life ten times easier for me.

I admired the guys who continued to go back to Iraq, the ones who did so and believed in the mission. I also admired the peace crowd, the people who cared enough about our country, and humanity, to get up and speak out. I, too, wanted to feel something, anything. Even if it meant turning my back on everything I had once believed in. I was all for growing my hair long and throwing two peace fingers in the air if I thought becoming a peacenik would help move me closer to an enlightenment of some sort.

When I got home, I read through the list of KIAs and asked myself, "Why are these troops dead? Why do so many of us have PTSD? Why am I so damned angry?" I'd heard so many people talk about how much we needed to be in Iraq. I heard people say that pulling out of the war would make the deaths that had already occurred be in vain. I was having a hard time following that line of thinking. How exactly could somebody actually believe that more death would honor the dead? To make things worse, most of the people advocating the war were doing so from the comfort of the United States. The old saying "Practice what you preach" came to mind.

I needed an explanation, someone to tell me that all the sacrifices were worth it, someone to justify the deaths that continued to accumulate and the pain felt by the men and women who'd managed to return. Most of all, I needed to be able to believe in something. I needed to find a warehouse chapel in the desert, a satchel of perfumed letters, or a lie I could buy into. Anything. Anything would've been better than nothing.

14

EVERYBODY IN THE WAITING room looked much younger. I wanted to believe it was some kind of fluke and we all just happened to be in the same room at the same time. But I knew that wasn't the case. It couldn't have been. VA mental health clinics around the country probably looked exactly like the Jade Clinic: filled to the brim with teenagers and twenty-somethings.

Was America ready for a brand-new batch of mentally impaired combat veterans? It didn't appear so.

The VA's motto is "To care for him who shall have borne the battle and for his widow, and his orphan." President Abraham Lincoln said that in 1865, during his second inaugural address. The U.S. government has had more than 140 years to live up to those words and still hasn't been able to get it right.

How many psychiatrists had I cycled through? Three or four? I couldn't remember. I did, however, know I could've filled in at the clinic had they needed me to. It didn't take a medical degree to ask a few stock questions, fill out a prescription, and then send someone on his way. I tried to remain optimistic. In the age of instant news and chest-pounding patriotism, Americans wouldn't allow anything but the best for their veterans. Americans love their vets. For proof, you only needed to stand on any street corner to see all of the support we were receiving in the form of Yellow Ribbon magnets the carport patriots had placed on the back of their gas-guzzling SUVs.

The problem could've been rectified had anyone *really* cared. Instead, we were forced to fend for ourselves, tossed into the failing VA system and made to endure all the red tape, hurry-up-and-wait it had to offer. Civilians were too busy worrying about celebrities to care; they thought lip service and bumper stickers would pacify us.

Who supports the troops? The troops support the troops.

A physician's assistant (PA) called me into his office. He offered me a seat when I walked in, then sat down in front of his computer. "I'll be with you in a second," he said. The routine felt familiar; I had gone through it six or seven times already.

Kipper appeared in the office. He was wearing a pair of

oil-stained, desert-camouflaged coveralls he'd found lying on the ground in Baghdad. They were two sizes too small for him, but he squeezed into them anyway and, before we left the country, could almost get the zipper pulled all the way to the top without having to suck in his stomach too much.

"What does this place remind you of?" I asked Kipper.

"Not sure, but I'm guessing it has something to do with Iraq."

"Remember the children's hospital my section went to guard? It was a couple of klicks or so from the main gate, to the west, I think. We camped inside the compound in order to keep the local scumbags from shooting it up at night."

"Okay. And?"

"Well, nothing happened. It was all hype."

"Sounds like something did happen, if nothing happened."

"Okay, riddler, I'll play your game. What do you mean?"

"Your job was to secure and protect the facility. If nobody shot it up that night, then the mission was successful. Right? You have to look at things in a different way sometimes. Even if you aren't getting the best treatment here, at least you're here. You are trying to change. That counts for something."

"Whatever," I said to Kipper.

"Excuse me," the PA replied.

It began to get hot in the room. Oven hot. Sweat dripped down my face. I slid a comm helmet onto my head, waited for the journey to begin, for the moment I would make my big getaway from reality.

"Stinky, this is Buckeye."

"Send it," I replied.

"Prepare to move out."

The PA finished typing. He swiveled his chair toward me, crossed his legs.

"Now, tell me about your experiences in Iraq."

Gunny's voice drifted through the comm helmet again. "Let's go," he said. "We've got a time hack to make."

"Negative," I said into the microphone. "I'm not going anywhere. I'm deadlined."

An hour passed. A full hour without being asked the usual list of questions, without having to repeat the same information I'd provided to the previous batch of nurses and doctors.

The rest of the staff in the crazy-man clinic seemed to view us as a nuisance. Not so with the PA. It was apparent he realized the importance of the work he was doing and how he had the ability to make a difference in veterans' lives. A few more people like him could've made a big difference, but one person wasn't going to be enough to even get through the guys that had been seated in that single waiting room. They'd have to deal with whatever half-assed psychiatrist they were given.

"See you in a few weeks, okay?" he said. "And don't hesitate to call if you need anything." He extended his business card.

"You won't be seeing me anytime soon. I'm moving to Wales in a few weeks. Going to Swansea for grad school."

"Well, make sure you stop by when you get back."

I'd finally found the one person in the crazy-man clinic who was willing to help. But it was too late. I wouldn't be around to clog the system any longer. They were free of me. I was free of them. It was time to move on, time to see a different part of the world, time to take control of my life.

The Marines taught me that if you want something to happen, *you* have to make it happen. It's called initiative. Sara and I were about to make stuff happen for us by moving out of the country. I wasn't giving up on the U.S.A., just taking a break, regrouping. I was going to get the chance to go back to the region I had looked down upon on Valentine's Day 2003, wondering if I would ever get to see the area again. My life was about to come full circle in so many ways.

15

Y OU ARE NOW LEAVING ARIZONA...

Technically, Sara and I were homeless. We'd stuffed a few suitcases full of clothes, sold almost everything else we owned, and bought one-way tickets to the United Kingdom. In the middle of packing and selling our possessions, Sara had decided to give up her perfectly fine surname for the much longer last name my father had passed down to me. We'd gotten married in an unceremonious ceremony at a local courthouse, used two clerks for witnesses, and then went back to getting rid of the rest of our stuff. Selling all of our belongings had a cleansing effect, made it seem like we were getting a fresh start on life. Unfortunately, our two dogs weren't invited to Wales; they were going to spend a year at my dad's house.

"Hope the dogs like Florida," Sara said.

Every once in a while one of the dogs would pop its head over the backseat or I'd catch a glimpse of a wagging tail. Our dogs would've been happy anywhere. I was envious.

"Hope we like Wales," I answered.

We were trading tacos for Welsh cakes, cactus-dotted mountains for lush green valleys, and bottles of cerveza for pints of Brains Smooth. Neither of us had ever been to Wales. The near flyover on the way to Iraq was the closest I'd been to the country. Still, I didn't have any doubts about going—my maternal roots had originated there, which made me feel that it was the place where I belonged at that point in my life. Back to the beginning. A reverse migration. Anyway, it couldn't have been any worse than some of the places I'd lived. Nobody would be shooting at us, and we wouldn't have to live outside or go without showers for a month. However, Wales would have to wait, at least for a month. We still had to visit family in Florida and Virginia before catching that freedom bird to Swansea.

Tourists crossed the street instead of walking by the VFW. Even in a city as bizarre as Key West, where just about anything goes, the bar was too eccentric for the masses of

Hawaiian-shirted tourists and beer-guzzling college students. The bar's patrons were a rough crowd, the people nobody else wanted to drink with. The Key West VFW bar felt like a scene out of a movie: Long-haired men with long beards shoveled down Fourth of July barbecue and cheap beer. Vietnam-era music blared from the jukebox. I might have been too young to be hanging out in such a place, but I felt much older, like I'd already lived through a lifetime's worth of experiences.

A one-legged man parked his wheelchair at the end of the bar and yelled into the palms of his hands that he was "back in Nam." He attempted to make a phone call through the end of his fingers. His nub bounced with the beat of the music. "A few more drinks," I said to myself, "and then we'll see where I wind up."

Nobody said anything about the exposed "Oorah" tattoos that covered my upper right arm, but I sensed that a few of the men were staring at them, sizing me up, and trying to figure out what I was all about. I inched closer to the bar, stared into the mirror that hung behind it, and watched myself drink. I *was* one of them: a drunk, crazy veteran. The idea didn't bother me anymore.

A loudmouth at the opposite end of the bar hollered something in my direction. I looked over, nodded, and then raised my mug of beer a few inches off the bar. He swaggered over in a matter-of-fact sort of way, like he knew something I didn't, like there was some sort of running joke between us and I owed him a drink.

"Hurrah," he said.

"What? You a cheerleader?"

"I did Vietnam," he said, failing to give any specifics.

"What was your MOS?"

Blank stare. No reply. He'd already showed his hand by saying "hurrah" instead of the Marine Corps "Oorah" or the Army "Hooah." While many of the people in the bar were vets of some sort, it was open to the public, which meant imposters were present. Seemed like the Hurrah Guy was trying to get a free drink out of me. But I wasn't bothered, too much, and let it slide. I hadn't gone to the VFW to play games or sip fruity drinks; I just wanted to spend Independence Day with the *real* veterans, the guys who might have known a thing or two about falling over the edge.

I shook my head, stood up, and walked to the other end of the bar without saying a word to the freeloader. At first, I had hoped my abrupt exit would offend him, hoped he would say something that would get me riled enough to crash a chair into his leathery face or pound his skull against the jukebox. Although it had been a long time since I'd punched anyone, I still had a lot of fight left in me and the Fourth of July seemed like the perfect time to end the dry spell. But what was the use? It wasn't a battle worth fighting.

Sara pulled up on a rented scooter. She walked in, draped her arms around my sunburnt neck, and kissed the side of my face. You could tell by the way the rest of the men in the bar looked at her that tall, tan, and blond didn't fit the description of the women who normally hung out in the establishment.

Having a full set of teeth certainly earned her a few bonus points.

"Are you doing all right?" she whispered into my ear.

"I can still hold on to my mug. So, yeah, I'm A-OK. But could you please do me a favor and drop some quarters in the jukebox? It's getting way too quiet in here."

"Sure. What do you want to hear?"

"Why don't we get drunk and screw," I sang to her.

"Is that a song or a proposition?" she asked.

"Both."

"Better try again."

"How about some Springsteen."

"Some what?"

"You don't know *who* I am talking about, do you?" I slurred. I'd forgotten that her knowledge of pop culture was zero and she really didn't have a clue. Sara wouldn't have made it very far on *Name That Tune*. "Play 'Born in the U.S.A.'"

Sara walked over to the jukebox. The men followed her with their eyes, watched her drop the quarters in and select the song. After a few seconds, the song came roaring out of the speakers. By the noise the crowd of drinkers made when they heard the song's opening synthesizer riff, the bar approved of the selection.

Sara slid a stool next to me. I moved my face close to hers, started singing the first verse with Bruce. A female bartender sang along as well. The barmaid looked over and smiled, brought another mug of beer. Sara put her hand on my lower back, leaned against me.

"Rickard."

"What?" Sara asked.

"Yes, Sergeant," Rickard answered.

"Turn the volume up," I said.

He pushed the volume button on the personal CD player we had jerry-rigged to the AAV's intercom by attaching a few wires to the CD player and then running them up to one of the radios. It wasn't a skill taught at AAV School, but something most trackers learned along the way. If you connected it correctly, the music would pipe in through the comm helmets. If you did it wrong, you ran the risk of playing your tunes across the platoon frequency every time you tried to communicate to the other vehicles, which would get you an ass chewing for sure. "Loud enough?" he asked.

The lyrics were lost on us. We didn't understand the song, didn't understand that it wasn't meant for what we were using it for. We just knew Bruce kept singing he was born in the U.S.A. over and over again. Although none of the Iraqis could hear the song as we blazed through their godforsaken city, playing it made us feel like we were giving them the finger— our last fuck-you. We were heading home.

The song repeated. Dust blew into our faces from the line of vehicles in front of us. Rickard and I bobbed our heads with the music. Lieutenant Frank, who wasn't happy when Rickard played a hip-hop album laced with lyrics that probably would have gotten three white guys like us in trouble had they been transmitted over the radio, could handle listening to Springsteen, and was bobbing his head to the beat as well.

Rickard steered the AAV down the road leading out of Baghdad, mindlessly following the caravan of AAVs. We only had a few more miles of war, only a few more miles. Bombed-out buildings and burnt homes blurred into one big strip of colors. We thought the war had ended for us, thought we would never have to see Iraq again.

Paxson answered after the third ring. I held my phone in the air so he could hear the jukebox.

"*I'm a long gone daddy in the U.S.A.*"

"Yo, happy Fourth," I yelled into the phone.

"Shit-ass," he replied. "You here yet?"

"Naw, bro, not until next week."

"I'll have some ice-cold beer waiting on you."

16

PAXSON AND I WERE sitting in plastic lawn chairs in his front yard, watching his two little boys play in an inflatable pool he had erected. He only had a few more days left in base housing before being kicked back into the civilian world after having spent the previous ten years of his life in the Corps. I knew he didn't want to leave, didn't want out of the Marines. But after numerous surgeries on his back, and several months of medical evaluations, he'd been told to pack his shit and hit the door. Thanks for playing. Game over.

Sitting in those lawn chairs, just a few miles from the Naval Amphibious Base where we had been stationed together, it was hard to imagine what kind of people we had been a few years earlier. Both of us had planned on retiring from the Marines, not leaving in our midtwenties.

"Do you have anything to do tomorrow?" I asked.

"Nope."

"Want to drink a few beers and take the canoe out?"

"I don't give a fuck. I'll canoe."

He pulled two more beers out of the cardboard container they came in, passed a can over to me. We chugged them and then tossed the crumpled cans into the soggy lawn. Pax reached into the case and grabbed another beer. "Last one." Beer foam splattered over his bare chest when he yanked the can's pop-top open. He leaned his head back, took a few gulps, and then passed it over to me.

"What now?" I asked.

"We could head over to the V-F-fucking-W."

"And get our swerve on?"

"You know it."

Pax used his knees to drive while he fiddled with the radio with one hand and rooted around in the center console with the other. He spat streams of chewing tobacco out of the window in between gulps from one of the two double deuces we'd just bought, yelled at the stereo when a song he didn't want to hear was played. It may have been dangerous, especially since neither of us was in any condition to drive, but together we felt invincible, like we were riding in amtracs again, looking for doors to kick in and people to shoot.

"What do you want to listen to?" he asked while sorting through a pile of his wife's CDs. "These are shit." He flung the ones he didn't like out of the open window, and then pulled out his cell phone. "Let's call Kipper," he said. I grabbed the steering wheel. He dialed. "Not answering. I'll try G-Money Yates." No answer again. He pressed the gas pedal to the floor. I steered into the next lane and down an off-ramp.

Bailey didn't answer his phone either. Pax called him a "dick wad" and then dialed another number. When he couldn't get Gunny Rines on the line, he punched in a few more numbers. The car swerved over the double line and we laughed and yelled into the wind. Kipper answered the second try. Paxson cussed at him, then threw the phone into my lap, took control of the steering wheel again. "Let me guess," Kipper said, "the Norfolk VFW."

It was a different VFW bar but basically the same. I knew why at least two people showed up to drink. Unlike the missions I often made to the Mexican restaurant in Phoenix, the bar stool patrons in the VFW seemed to recognize our mission as soon as we walked in and nobody said anything to us as we continually violated the bar's no cussing policy. It helped out that Pax frequented the establishment and was wearing a mesh, trucker-style Norfolk VFW hat to prove it.

A guy leaning against the end of the bar shook our hands when we walked into the smoke-filled room and told the bartender to put our first round of drinks on his tab. We ordered two pitchers of beer, talked with the old-timer for a few minutes before moving to a table in the back.

For once, I didn't feel so crazy. I didn't think about the outside world or the fact that I'd promised Sara I would be home two hours earlier, sober. She knew what I was up to and what to expect once I got around another Marine, especially one I'd served with. My mind stayed in the present. There wasn't any need to drift into the past, no reason to take another mental voyage.

We sat at a table in the corner, our sweat-stained desert cammies invisible to everyone else.

"Think it was worth it?" I asked.

"Does it matter?" he answered.

I returned home drunk and began to tell Sara about the war, nothing too detailed, just the mundane parts. I didn't mention the dead children or burnt bodies or the way the remains of the dead Marine looked lying in the dirt moments before we left him. I said nothing about the way it felt to have to prepare for death or how I had actually enjoyed shooting at one point. The alcohol wanted me to tell her, wanted her to know all about the war, what it was really like, and why I continually thought about it. I could have told her anything, but never was able to muster up the courage to talk about my experiences, about the little girl or the reason I woke up disoriented whenever I did manage to fall asleep.

Sara couldn't have been sure whether it was Sergeant Van

Winkle or Clint lying beside her or what combination of the two had stumbled into bed with her. She probably didn't want to hear about the war anyway, didn't want to relive the good ol' times I spent in Iraq or hear stories about Kipper's legendary "Track Turkey" scrotum or Paxson's "Flying Squirrel" ball-sack or Bailey's "helicopter" dick trick. The years since I'd been home had been hard on her, too, and I bet she would've liked to have forgotten about the whole ordeal and moved on with our lives. She listened anyway. Not because she was afraid of me but because it seemed like she knew that's what I needed: someone to tell my story to, someone who would listen and care that war had taken a toll on my friends and me.

I watched the ceiling fan spin. Sara caressed the top of my head. I knew drinking wasn't helping anything. It never had. Alcohol couldn't earn repentance, couldn't cover up the scars or change anything that I'd done. It was as useless as any of the pills the doctors had tried to shove down my throat. No matter what I did, I would still be a killer, a wife abuser, and a fucked-up veteran with PTSD.

Everything is going to be okay, I thought. I can do this. I won't end up washing windows in the blazing heat or yelling into the palm of my hands at an island VFW or patrolling alleys in search of a war that is physically over for me. Tomorrow's a new day. I'll start to get things together.

"I'm sorry," I mumbled.

"It's not your fault," she said.

It really wasn't my fault. I knew that. But rationalizing war was like trying to count stars on a cloudy night. There wasn't any use or sense to it. Still, I had been trying to unearth the meaning, even though I knew there wasn't a meaning. There never was, never will be. I told myself all of that and promised I wouldn't think about the war anymore. It didn't matter how hard I tried, there wasn't anything I could do to make it all go away.

War becomes a part of you. It is a feeling just as much as an experience. If you can't feel it, you weren't paying attention. And if you weren't paying attention, you are probably dead anyway. Things like PTSD made me human, a reminder that I was still capable of feeling, even if the feeling was mainly anger.

The thumping of the ceiling fan sounded like a low-flying Black Hawk. Cool desert air blasted onto my sweaty face. I drifted in and out of consciousness, watched the scattered light of tracer rounds pierce the dark's thickness. The feelings encompassed my body, fresh as yesterday.

From the darkness, a voice called me away from the protection of my two machine guns. It was Gunny. He stood outside my vehicle, his tan and brown camouflage helmet unstrapped, clutching an M16. Incoming rounds flashed by him, but he didn't move. His calmness let me know everything was going to be okay. "Let's go," he said.

I walked through the battlefield with him, to a vehicle whose luck was different than mine. It sat a mere twenty yards away, twisted and dead, its aluminum hull crunched up like a discarded beer can. "Get in," he ordered. He pointed to the wreck with his rifle. "We need the parts."

I obeyed and climbed in.

The inside of the AAV, once sea-foam green, was charred black, its wounds all too evident. I stepped over body parts and shredded uniforms, tried to make my way to what was left of the turret. My boots made a squishing sound against the sticky floor as I moved forward through the torn-up troop compartment. It was obvious the war hadn't gone so well for the Marines who had been riding in the vehicle, but I had a mission to accomplish and kept moving.

"It's all fucked up. No parts," I yelled.

"All right, you're done," Gunny replied.

That simple. He got me, I listened, no parts, I left. But nothing in war is simple.

I didn't take anything, left only a shard of my soul. Each step I took caused dirt to shoot up into small clouds. But the clouds ceased momentarily, gave way to an unfamiliar feeling beneath my boots—a soft spot on the hard ground. It was a mere change in texture, nothing more.

The warmth of the morning sun replaced the darkness, revealed the destruction we caused, the death we created. Gunshots still raced about the area, mainly outgoing. Short bursts from automatic weapons, a little yelling. Some were shooting at shadows, others at imaginary people lurking in windows.

A convoy sped through the safety of the morning light and sent a curtain of dust over the battlefield. They were support guys, and their only connections to combat were our radio communications, our gunfire, and our wreck of a city. Through the dust, they stared at the twisted heap that had been an amphibious assault vehicle a few hours earlier. Like a before-and-after picture, one wrecked vehicle parked directly next to my whole, untouched vehicle. Luck of the draw.

Tired Marines in desert camouflage were scattered on the hard ground, still defending the road for the convoys. Marines in the passing trucks pointed toward the soft spot. Their faces seemed horrified, like they had witnessed something they'll never forget. I told myself not to look, to change direction, think of something else. "You've seen it before," I said to myself. I looked down anyway, reconfirmed the images already stuck in my head.

The soft spot was still present. He had been a change in texture, nothing more.

Each night, images of the dead looped through my thoughts, revealed forgotten details. Hidden details that lay dormant until the body was relaxed enough to accept them. The magician of the mind would pull them out, surprise the audience.

I could see Gunny's face, his harsh expression crumbling into grief for the battered body I had stepped on, and could feel my boot sinking into the remains of the Marine. The Marines in the convoy parted back the curtain of dust so they could watch the show, stare at the carnage that was yards from me. A viewing for the dead.

The shaking of a dog chain tore me away from the war. Large red numbers on a small black alarm clock illuminated the room, indicating it was two A.M. My yellow Lab stretched her head up from below and nudged my arm. I turned over. Pulled a white down comforter above my head, returned to war.

The horizon was without trees or buildings as the sun fell into the earth again. Purples and reds bled into the dirt. The colors were beautiful. So much beauty. So much destruction.

Paxson, Kipper, and I took lawn chairs out of a vehicle. We plopped down and stretched our legs out, let the oncoming darkness wrap around us. Nobody knew where to begin or what to talk about. So, to keep sane we talked about combat like it was some kind of joke.

"Does it count as a kill if you run over a dead Iraqi?"

"Hell yeah, that's a rekill!"

We laughed. Wives at home fucking neighbors, our corpsman shooting a dog, and rekills—that had become our humor.

The joking ceased after I climbed into my sleeping bag and reality emerged. Bullets began their nightly parade through the sky, zigzagging, looking for a human home. The dead resurrected to show their faces. Peace surfaced here. Hard to imagine a person finding peace through war, but no one finds peace in war—peace finds you. It crawls into your sleeping bag and helps you fall asleep, nudges your arm, tells you to turn over, think about home. I pulled the black Gore-Tex sleeping bag above my head to cover the sight of the dead children, mask the bitter smell of burnt flesh, and transported myself home.

Traveling between home and war made it hard to know where reality lay. Were they dreams of home or war? It was blurred. The ceiling fan thumped, the ground shook, tracer rounds zipped by my face, and the deception of dreams continued.

The story goes something like that, but I can't locate its actual truth. Truth lives where that piece of my soul once did and visits me briefly in sleep—only to disappear with waking. Gunfire, destroyed vehicles, dead Marines, and Iraq are the truth. The rest is equivocal. Everything appears to me vaguely or in fragments. I guess that's how war is: It simply happens and the pieces never fit together. The mind numbs, so you can look at the dead, kill the living. It keeps the absolute truth just out of reach, allowing you to march on—even through the soft spots.

17

FOUR ICE-COLD CANS OF beer rolled around the hull of a yellow, two-man canoe as Paxson and I pushed the fiberglass craft off a muddy bank and into the slow-moving brown water. We were lost in our own world, drinking away our VFW hangovers. The sounds of coolers creaking open and party jokes faded with each paddle stroke. We paddled like it was a formation run, in sync, but to our own cadence. The sight of bonfire flames only accompanied us so far, and then we were on our own, in the middle of a small offshoot of the Atlantic Intercostal Waterway, drunk and without life jackets. Paxson's empty beer can hit the bottom of the canoe like a spent .50-cal casing. I chugged to catch up. Opened another with him. We laughed, paddled, drank, and talked.

Pax and I hashed out our versions of stories and neither version was alike. Each story, however, spurred another—propelled the canoe farther down the creek. We chewed the same dirt together, yet we were unable to find a common story, an identical account. I wanted to tell him I had been scared that I would get one of my Marines killed. I wanted to tell him I thought we were going to die and that maybe we should have. I didn't, though. As usual, I said nothing. The paddle strokes slowed between stories and sips of beer. A swarm of Canadian geese hollered from behind a cluster of reeds. Pax seemed to know what I wanted to say, and I could tell he wanted to say the same thing. In telling our stories we revived our death letters. Turned out they were as much for us as for our loved ones.

I have the serial numbers to every rifle and gas mask of every Marine in third section scribbled in the front pages of my Death Journal. Ticked, checked, and marked off, I know these are accurate. I know Lance Corporal "Hammer Toe" Reed wore a pair of black combat boots two sizes too small and needed a new pair. I'm still not sure why he wore a pair of boots that didn't fit, or why he waited until we arrived in Kuwait to tell anyone about the size discrepancy, but do know that a few days before we crossed over into Iraq, Gunny managed to get him a pair of boots that fit. I know which Marines lost rounds and how many I had to acquire to fix the deficiency. It's all there, written down in my green notebook. But when I get to the back, to the death journal portion, I don't trust anything I'd written. I can't trust anything. The words are jumbled ink blots of half-truths. It is the space between those portions, between the serial numbers and death journal, I am attempting to fill now. The same space I've been stuck in since returning home: between the wrong and right, that first day in Kuwait and the present, the firefights and canoe trips.

EPILOGUE

An INDEX AND MIDDLE finger are slowly moving in front of my face, back and forth, at a distance we agreed would be comfortable for me. I track the fingers with my eyes, prepare for the ride the new-wave therapy is about to induce. This is the Phoenix Vet Center, the Special Forces of the VA system, a place I wish somebody would've told me about years ago. I'd managed to get through graduate school in Wales with very little stress. However, the return to Phoenix, with its four million people, bumper-to-bumper traffic, anthill congestion, and desert landscape, had the reverse effect.

Kipper ran his life into a mud hole, too. I knew before leaving the country that he hadn't been doing well either, couldn't get the war off his mind, but I didn't know the extent of his struggle. He'd gotten bad, and by the time I returned from Wales, he was in a full tailspin, about to crash and burn. And while Swansea helped me in the healing process, I still wasn't where I needed to be either. Chaos still controlled my mind. Iraq still occupied much of my time and spilled over into everything I did. It was time to let go of the past, for real this time, and break out of the chains that bound us. Kipper and I made a pact to straighten our lives out, to regain control. We'd do it together, make sure neither got left behind, and also try to get Paxson on board before he ended up using the 12-gauge tactical shotgun he often carried around Philly with him.

So here I am. Sitting in a large office, watching two fingers pass by my face in a process called eye movement desensitization and reprocessing (EMDR), a controversial form of psychotherapy being used on PTSD patients. The man moving his fingers in front of my face is Joseph Little, MSW, a readjustment counselor and team leader of the Phoenix Vet Center. Joe is a combat vet, too. He stops his hands, tells me to take a deep breath, and then asks, "What do you get now?"

"Swansea, Wales," I say.

"Go with that," Joe says.

I start laughing, not because anything is funny but because I am nervous. "You'll be fine. Keep going," Joe says. I have unconditional trust in this man, which is why I decided to let him perform EMDR on me even though many psychologists question the therapy's validity. But what do psychologists really know about war trauma unless they've experienced it? I'd been to a slew of "mind" doctors, and look where that got me. Joe is different, knows more about combat veterans than all of the skeptical psychologists combined. He's mentioned some of his experiences as an LRRP and a Ranger Special Ops team leader in Vietnam, but what he isn't aware of is that I know more about his past than what he's told me. Even though he would never claim the title, Joe is a bona fide war hero and has more medals for valor than anybody I've ever met: Two Silver Stars, a handful of Bronze Stars, and three Purple Hearts are a few of the medals I remember seeing in a picture of a much younger Sergeant Little. The knowledge Joe has about war can't be learned in college courses. There isn't anything I can say that he won't understand, and I never have to give full-on explanations when talking to him. We're connected by war, the pain it has caused. Talking to him is like talking to Kipper or Paxson.

His fingers pass in front my face again. I follow them; return to the place that relaxes me the most.

A radiator on the far side of the room crackles as hot water circulates through its steel coils. Sara and I sip Earl Grey and watch the beam of light shining from the Mumbles lighthouse break through a drizzle of rain. We're waiting for the sun to appear from behind the rolling green hills, waiting to see the bay sparkle in the morning light. A large floor-to-ceiling bay window on the third story of our semidetached Victorian offers breathtaking views of Swansea Bay, and we spend countless hours watching the ebb and flow of the bay, the ever-present rain, and of course, the lighthouse. Sara leans over and kisses me. She gathers our empty mugs and goes downstairs to our galley-style kitchen. We both have morning classes and, since walking has been our only means of transportation, will have to leave our flat soon. I slide on my boots, gather my books, and then meet Sara in the kitchen.

Sara and I walk briskly down the winding, rain-drenched streets, through the village of Sketty toward Swansea University. She clutches the top of my arm with her gloved hand, leans into my body. The walk to school is one of the best parts about living in Sketty.

After passing the bakery, we cross Gower Road, where St. Paul's Church stands on the corner. The stone building, complete with bell tower, is surrounded by 150 years' worth of graves and marks the point where we enter Singleton Park. From the top of the hill we can see the university's campus, which is nestled between the park and Swansea Bay. Tranquil *and* relaxing *don't do the scenery justice.*

The sight is beyond beautiful.

My mind is somewhere between the sprawling green park and Swansea Bay when Joe speeds the movement of his fingers. The rain stops. Greenery bleeds into a tan and brown desert. My clothes transform into a set of camouflage cammies and all of a sudden I can feel the weight of a Flak jacket wrapped around my torso.

"Take a deep breath," Joe says. "What do you get now?"

"I was in the park," I say. "But now I'm carrying a rifle."

"It's okay. Go with that."

EMDR is user centered. The therapist lets you control your thoughts, and only steps in if it starts to get too rough in your head. We're taking it slow, working our way into full-on war memories. When we get to that point, my neurotransmitters will be firing at the cyclic rate of a .50 cal and Joe might have to guide my mind back to Wales. But for now I am doing okay. I'm ready to move forward.

Deep breath. Concentrate. Relax.

I shift on the leather couch, squeeze my eyes shut for a minute, and then open them again. I track Joe's fingers. The park in Swansea shows itself for a split second, then fades to black.

Rickard gives a thumbs-up when I look back. He spins the turret, orders Meyers to inch the vehicle closer to the squad of grunts I am patrolling the streets with. I know the weapons in the turret are clean and in good working order but am not too sure about the rifle I borrowed from Meyers. If we get into a firefight, I'll find out. Even though my pistol is strapped across my chest, and is immaculate, the 9-mil won't do much good unless we get up close and personal with the enemy. The grunts move forward, past one crumbling home and one that is in only slightly better condition. I follow. I don't have any reason for being on the ground, and should be in the turret, controlling the section, but Hall is competent, maybe more than I am, so I don't have much to worry about except for the fact that I might be carrying a screwed-up rifle and that I put a private first class in charge of the AAV. A quick calculation reminds me that Rickard was still in middle school when I was a recruit in boot camp.

A burst of gunfire and we are running. Rickard has Meyers move the AAV behind a building, so only the top of the turret is visible. It was a good decision and I'm surprised he thought of it so quickly. But then, combat doesn't take a lot of thinking, just a lot of reacting, and we've been doing the same thing for so long that it is just the natural thing to do: find a safe place and prepare to shoot. He doesn't fire, though, which is a good thing, since there are civilians scattered around the area.

I'm lying in the prone position, alongside the rest of the grunts, behind a small mound of dirt in the middle of an empty field. Looking around, I realize that the only thing green within eyeshot is the olive drab Nomex jumpsuit I'm wearing. Sore thumb, hell, I'm sticking out like a burning bush. I don't remember how we got here, but since I am breathing pretty hard, I know we got here fast. The grunt squad leader pulls at his sleeve and tells us to look at his goddamned uniform. He says the rip came from the burst of rounds fired at us. He's pretty pissed, mainly because he'll have to sew it up when we get back to the warehouse complex, but also because he didn't get a chance to return fire and kill the pricks who caused it. However, he says we are about to change all of that and tells us to prepare for a squad rush. A four-story building across the field is our objective and is surrounded by a six-foot-high block wall. Whoever tried to kill us fired his weapon from behind the wall, we think.

A grunt corporal I've been calling "Rocket Man" because of all the rockets he carries wants to launch an AT4 into the building, and asks for permission to fire into the wall. He spends a lot more time asking permission to launch the expensive rockets he's been lugging around than he gets to actually fire them. I'm not too sure he hasn't managed to squeeze a few off when nobody's been looking, but if he has, only the CO would care. We like to see shit blow up.

Meyers's rifle is pressed into my shoulder and I am running across the open field. It's a dead sprint. I hurdle chunks of buildings and stray rocks. We stop at the wall, hoist one man up so he can see over, and follow it around to the front of the building.

Men are moving supplies out of the building, mostly foodstuffs, and we tell them to get the fuck back. Rickard followed us in the AAV and has it positioned a few feet away from the entrance. He spins the turret into the crowd of people, lowers the weapons. I nod my head at him, happy that he's learned so much since we've been in Iraq, that he's picked up on the art of intimidation and is capable of patrolling without much guidance. I wave him closer and then walk back to meet him halfway.

"Is this good, Sergeant?" he asks when I get to the side of the vehicle.

"Call Hall if anything goes down," I yell up to him. "I'm going in."

Two of the grunts stay by the building's entrance. Two more stay with the AAV. The rest of us file in through a heavy wood door, separate into fire teams, and begin to clear the building. I have my rifle pointed up, toward the second story as we move up a set of stairs. When we get to the second level, we start kicking in doors.

Joe stops his fingers.

"Are you okay?" he asks.

"That was intense," I say. "More vivid than any dream I've ever had. Unbelievable clarity. Not only could I see and feel the places, I was able to make sense out of what I was going through. I've never been able to process anything completely, but then, instantaneously I could. Why is that?"

Why EMDR works, nobody really knows. Even practitioners have problems explaining the results they see in their patients. It's possible that the process of watching fingers move side to side evokes some sort of placebo effect where patients just think things are getting better, wishing so hard for positive results that they actually feel they have found one in EMDR. Placebo, wishful thinking, whatever. I'll take the help where I can get it.

It'll take another two or three sessions to complete the process. A matter of weeks will bandage the wound that has been oozing for four years. It seems too good to be true. But I can feel it working. My body seems lighter, my mind much clearer.

Second session. My eyes are closed and I am holding small tactile sensors in each hand. A pair of earphones sends alternating, rhythmic thuds into my ears, making it sound like an electronic Ping-Pong game is taking place. Oddly enough, the eye movement (the basis, and namesake, of the psychotherapy) has been taken out of the EMDR equation. Joe controls the sounds via remote control, adjusts the rate of speed accordingly. The sensors buzz in sync with the earphones. Left, right, left, right.

"Start in Wales," Joe says. We've decided that this is my place of comfort, and since it is best to ease into the traumatic scenes, that's where he wants me to begin. I try to go back to Swansea, to the sprawling park that borders the university, but my mind is leading my thoughts to another country.

Sara and I are walking together, close enough that I will be able to throw her out of the way if an explosion occurs or knock a weapon out of someone's hands if we are attacked. I'm beyond hypervigilant and have been looking for suicide bombers since we arrived in Tunisia. It isn't really like Iraq, but the predominantly Muslim North African country resembles Iraq enough to make the vacation feel more like a combat tour than a week relaxing at a cozy resort on the Mediterranean Sea.

It was my idea to spend a week of our Christmas vacation in Sousse, Tunisia, and each day I've regretted making the reservations. I've wanted to fly back to Wales ever since arriving. But Sara loves the place and is intrigued with the culture. Besides, her family is Lebanese, and the locals look like they could be her cousins. She tells me not to worry, that we are safe. I tell her there isn't any way I am not going to worry. Had she been shot at by people who looked exactly the same, while fighting in a similar country, she would be nervous, too. I try not to ruin her holiday but tell her to watch out for suspicious packages or big piles of trash.

"These are your people," I say to her.

"Watch your wallet," she responds.

A man in tattered clothes walks out from behind a wall. I can tell by the looks of him that he must also smell pretty bad. I keep my eyes on the Tunisian man but try not to make it too obvious. Neither Sara nor I is in any position to get into trouble with the law. Besides the fact that we're Americans, which I am sure the locals love, the armful of Marine Corps tattoos on my upper-right biceps probably wouldn't go over well if they were revealed.

The thought of Sara being hauled off to a third-world jail while I am being beaten by locals is running through my mind when the dirty-looking man gets within arm's reach of Sara. He lunges.

The motherfucker pushes my wife. I reach over and catch her arm as she stumbles into the street. Pulling on Sara's arm while speeding up my pace causes her to swing like a pendulum away from the trouble. We keep moving down the road, away from the son of a bitch. All of a sudden, I am back on patrol, for real. My head is on a swivel, looking for the next threat. Still, I am remarkably calm. It is the small things that piss me off. The big events I can handle. Sara is shaken, though, her eyes red. She's strong and won't cry in front of anybody, but once I get her into a taxi, all bets are off. The urge to kill a person is stronger than ever. Never have I felt so helpless. Never.

I open my eyes, stare at the office wall. An emotion other than anger is present. I can't remember the last time I cried, but a river seems poised to break through the dam. It might be time to purge the system and cleanse those tear ducts. I've got more discipline than that, however, and won't cry, but it's going to take a little effort.

Deep breath. Hard exhale.

"Go with it." I squeeze my eyes shut again, concentrate on the heartbeat rhythm and pulsing tactile sensors. I can't stop thinking about all the shit Sara has put up with and how I kept assuming I was alone when I really wasn't. How could I have felt so lonely when I had so many people trying to keep me from hitting the ground, attempting to pull my arm away from the craziness all along?

I'm sitting in front of my computer, watching the cursor blink. This is the final page of my first book and I desperately want to find a way to wrap it all up in a neat little package, find a happy ending to the last few hundred pages of misery. I'd like to be able to say I am cured because of EMDR, but I know better. It isn't that easy. The vivid memories I collected in combat won't disappear. A piece of me will always be in Iraq.